The Power of Meditation for ADHD

A Guide to Managing ADHD Symptoms with Mindful Meditation

by

E.V. Durand

BOOKS

About the Author

E.V. Durand

E.V. Durand is a psychiatric nurse practitioner who is driven by a deep passion to help individuals facing mental health challenges thrive in all aspects of their lives, regardless of their diagnosis. With extensive psychiatric experience, she has gained a comprehensive understanding of health, embracing the integration of cutting-edge pharmaceutical therapies and behavioral approaches for holistic well-being.

E.V. Durand's particular interest lies in attention deficit/hyperactivity disorder (ADHD), as she has witnessed firsthand the detrimental effects of this often-misunderstood condition. Believing in the transformative power of access to the right medications, resources, and meditative practices, her hope is that this book will open doors, shift perspectives, and ultimately enhance the quality of life for those impacted by ADHD.

Table of Contents

Introduction

Y ou've seen the memes and social media comments. *My ADHD could never* or, *That ADHD struggle*; an image of the Scooby Doo gang catching a ne'er-do-well villain in disguise labeled *ANXIETY & DEPRESSION*, only to unmask them and reveal their true identity as *UNDIAGNOSED ADHD*. Indeed, Attention Deficit Hyperactivity Disorder, or ADHD, has arrived in the mainstream, and it's of absolutely no surprise when one takes a peek at the numbers.

ADHD is the single most commonly diagnosed developmental disorder in children ages two to seventeen years old. According to the organization Children and Adults with Attention Deficit/Hyperactivity Disorder

(CHADD), a whopping 80% of them will experience symptoms into adulthood. This means that over eight million Americans (or 4% of the population) have been clinically diagnosed with ADHD. Further, recent studies suggest that percentage vastly underrepresented the true number, with most researchers extrapolating that it could be as high as 20% of the adult population – or over fifty-one million people.

That is a staggering number of people who live day in and day out with a disorder that can be debilitating in its ability to leech their focus and drive, deregulate control over their emotions, and increase impulsivity and hyperactivity. These symptoms can and do affect every area of a person's life; those with ADHD are four times more likely to experience clinical depression, anxiety disorders, and sleep disorders. They are half as likely to hold a steady job. They are more likely to struggle in relationships, and report more instances of negative self-talk than those without the disorder.

Luckily, there has been a recent explosion in the clinical research surrounding ADHD. One area of study focuses on symptom management, and recent research has sought to understand the role that things such as diet, exercise, and other lifestyle factors play in the presence and severity of ADHD symptoms.

Particularly exciting, and the focus of this book, is the transformative power of meditation as an approach to managing even the most severe of ADHD symptoms. In the coming chapters, we will provide a practical guide of techniques and resources to help individuals with ADHD harness the benefits of meditation and cultivate a calmer and more focused mind — all with the scientific research to back it up.

Living with ADHD can be demoralizing and a struggle, but it certainly does not have to be. By the end of this book, you will have the tools and resources to take control of your life and live with less stress, a less chaotic mind, and more peace.

Chapter 1
Understanding ADHD & its Challenges

W hat is ADHD? Most people understand it as a disorder that makes people forgetful, or at times hyperactive. While these are certainly common symptoms of the disorder, they do not explain what ADHD actually is, its effect on the brain, or even scratch the surface of how it can impact a person's life.

THE SCIENCEY STUFF

Attention Deficit/Hyperactivity Disorder is a developmental disorder, which is a disorder that affects the brain before the frontal lobe has fully developed. To be categorized as a developmental disorder three criteria have to be met: 1) the condition is apparent in an individual by age twenty-two, 2) the condition is chronic, and likely to continue throughout the individual's life, and 3) the condition adversely impacts at least three major areas of the individual's life.

In the case of ADHD, the first two criteria are easily met; most individuals diagnosed with ADHD can trace symptoms back to early adolescence or childhood, and in fact the American Psychiatrist Association requires that a person experience symptoms by age twelve in order to be clinically diagnosed with ADHD. As discussed in the introduction, 80% of those diagnosed with the disorder will continue to have symptoms into adulthood. But what *is* the disorder? *How* does it influence the brain? And how are these influences translated into symptoms and behaviors?

Physiologically, ADHD is defined by low levels of neurotransmitters in the brain; namely ***dopamine***, which is produced deep within the brain's center, and ***norepinephrine***, which is made from nerve endings produced in the brain stem. Neurotransmitters are essentially the brain's way of communicating with itself and the body. For example, say you hit your funny bone against the corner of your desk. The nerve in your elbow sends a message up your spinal cord to your brain stem, where neurotransmitters carry the message to the areas of your brain that perceive pain. The message is processed, and the sensation of pain is felt physically in the body. Obviously, this all happens in less than a single blink of the eye. In a brain that produces the typical or standard amounts of appropriate neurotransmitters, the regulation and processing of physical pain is normal. However, if the body does not produce enough neurotransmitters, dysregulation happens and can result in disorders such as Chronic Pain Syndrome.

In the case of ADHD, the low levels of dopamine and norepinephrine will affect how four major areas of the brain function and communicate with each other. The first is the ***frontal cortex***. The frontal cortex is made up of two lobes, spanning the hemispheres of the brain. They are the largest lobes and make up the biggest region of the brain and as the name suggests, are located in the front of the brain, directly behind your forehead. The frontal cortex regulates our attention, the ability to multitask, and plan ahead. This area is also responsible for our working memory, which allows us to process and use information simultaneously while not losing track of what we're doing.

This set of skills is known as **executive function** and generally speaking, we employ them without thinking about it. If you have ever signed your name, driven somewhere on "auto-pilot", listed off your phone number, or carried on a conversation while cleaning the kitchen, you used your executive function toolkit to do so. It is a vital part of daily life, and when the frontal cortex is dysregulated due to a lack of neurotransmitters, **executive dysfunction** occurs. Executive dysfunction is the most commonly reported symptom of those with ADHD and is known as **inattentive presentation**. It is also the one that many find to be the most frustrating due to its profound impact on daily life.

The second area of the brain that is adversely affected by ADHD is the **limbic system**. The limbic system is a cluster of structures that are located more or less within the center of the brain, and spreading down to the brain stem. The limbic system is responsible for **emotional regulation** within the brain, both intuitively by activating our more primal fight, flight, or freeze responses, and by helping us process new, more complicated emotions.

Low levels of dopamine can cause a breakdown in communication between the amygdala (a structure known as the emotional hub of the brain) and the limbic system. This breakdown can cause high levels of anger or shame, will oftentimes lead to destructive coping mechanisms, and can cause a person to suffer from depression and anxiety. Indeed, about 70% of adults with ADHD will experience severe depression in their lifetime.

The ***basal ganglia*** is a group of brain cells and nerves located in the center of the brain that are responsible for forming the connections, or neural pathways, that allow different areas of the brain to talk to each other. These pathways help temper impulsive behaviors, and when not functioning correctly, an individual with a lack of ***impulse control*** can be prone to impatience, poor or rash decision making, and escalating small problems into bigger issues. These reactive behaviors can result in self-medication in the form of substance abuse, self-harm, highly combative interpersonal relationships, and extremely psychologically damaging levels of perfectionism. A lack of impulse control is also associated with high levels of indulgence in anything from eating to shopping to gambling. It's the reason why many of those with ADHD (either diagnosed or not) consider themselves to have "addictive personalities."

Finally, the ***reticular activating system*** is a group of nerves that lies in the brain stem and modulates behavior. It does this by controlling any incoming stimuli and deciding what you should be aware of, and motivates you to react in certain ways. For example, you might accidentally touch a hot stove while scrolling social media on your phone. Your reticular activating system prioritizes the sensation of pain over stimulation of Instagram in order to get you to stop touching the stove.

Poor communication output to the rest of the brain from the reticular activating system can increase ***hyperactivity*** and has also been found to have an impact on sleep. If someone is constantly moving or talking, even in inappropriate situations, or has trouble falling and staying asleep at night, this could be a sign of low neurotransmission from the reticular activating system.

Obviously, no one wants to be fidgety, impulsive, scatterbrained, moody, tired and depressed. Just one of these symptoms of low levels of neurotransmission would be difficult to live with, but to attempt to navigate life with all of them can be debilitating. A study published in *Innovations in Clinical Neuroscience* found that adults with ADHD report having significantly less enjoyment of life and significantly less contentment when compared to adults without the disorder, and that symptoms resulted in low self-esteem and low self-confidence (Agarwal et al., 2012).

While the overall impact of these symptoms will certainly vary from person to person, it is agreed that they do affect every area of life. Children with ADHD as young as five years old find it difficult to make friends, have strained relationships with siblings, and difficulty connecting with their parents (Peasgood, 2016). Adults with the disorder find work tasks challenging and time management difficult, which can correlate to more mistakes on the job, more missed days, bad relationships with colleagues, and more suspensions and terminations. Further, "individuals with untreated ADHD have higher rates of unemployment and frequent job changes, and often are overlooked for higher-paying positions" (Janove, 2020, para. 5). People of all ages are nearly three times as likely to suffer from severe depression and anxiety, and those depressive and anxious symptoms are oftentimes felt more acutely in those with ADHD than in those without (Sherman, 2022, para. 2).

TREATMENT VIA MEDICATION

Luckily, there are pharmaceutical options that can be discussed with a physician once someone is diagnosed. These options fall into two categories: stimulants and non-stimulants. We won't spend too much time discussing these types of medications, but it's important to understand their functions and side effects.

Stimulant medications are made up of primarily two molecules that *stimulate* the central nervous system in the brain (hence the name) and convince it to speed up dopamine and norepinephrine messaging. While this doesn't increase the production of these neurotransmitters, it does result in improved executive and attention function. Stimulants can be prescribed in fast-acting pills that work from anywhere between three and six hours, and time-release formulas that stay in the body for up to twelve hours. 80% of medicated ADHD patients take some kind of stimulant, and there are many on the market, the two most often prescribed being Adderall and Ritalin. The success of a stimulant is dependent entirely on a person's brain chemistry, and will vary wildly from person to person.

The side effects of stimulants are also varied and can be as mild as a slight dizziness and a decrease in appetite, to more severe migraines and high blood pressure. There is also the risk of dependency. Some health conditions prohibit a person from taking stimulants, and so it's extremely important to discuss treatment plans with a qualified professional who knows your medical history.

A non-stimulant works by increasing the production of norepinephrine and, to a lesser extent, dopamine. About

20% of medicated ADHD patients take some form of atomoxetine, guanfacine, and clonidine, which all fall under the umbrella of non-stimulant medication. The vast majority of those who take non-stimulants do so because stimulants were proven to be ineffective in treating their ADHD symptoms, but there are a number of reasons why someone might prefer a non-stimulant option. Many people like the fact that non-stimulants are not habit-forming, and parents are oftentimes more comfortable putting their kids on non-stimulant medication for this reason.

The aforementioned three medications were for many years the only non-stimulants approved for market. Recently, however, for the first time in two decades, a new non-stimulant was deemed safe and effective by the FDA. Viloxazine (band name Qelbree), has been approved by adults, adolescents, and even children as young as six years old. It yields great results for ADHD symptom management.

It's important to note that non-stimulants need to be taken for a number of weeks to "build up" in the central nervous system before the intended effects can be felt. This can make it frustrating and time consuming to find the correct medication and dosage. Much like stimulants, the success of these medications are dependent entirely upon individual brain chemistry.

Still, non-stimulants have side effects. These can include extreme fatigue, extreme weight fluctuation, mood swings, and nausea. Speaking with a physician about these and other side effects is the best course of action when making the decision to try non-stimulant medications.

While pharmaceuticals are a great tool in managing the symptoms of ADHD, there is another way to increase focus and emotional regulation, curb impulsivity and hyperactivity, and even improve sleep. When used in conjunction with medication, it becomes a powerful mechanism in improving the quality of life for so many with attention deficit/hyperactivity disorder.

In the next chapters we will discuss the transforming and restorative power of meditation.

Chapter 2
An Introduction to Meditation

M uch like ADHD, meditation has been a buzzword lately, thanks in part to a trendy emphasis on the idea of "self care," or taking time out to focus on one's own physical and mental health. Like many ideas and practices that are commodified for a quick buck, the core values and beliefs behind meditation have become somewhat perverted in order to be packaged for a shallow idea of "wellness". In this chapter we will dive deeper in order to understand what meditation is, where it originated, and ways it can be used in modern life.

WHAT IS MEDITATION?

Meditation is, in the simplest of terms, the cultivation of a quiet mind.

In our modern society, we are moving always at a frenetic pace. Whether it is hustling to and from jobs, trying to keep up with the Joneses, the incessant scrolling and addiction to technology, or the demands of ever more involved societal expectations, we rarely hit the pause button. This breakneck, non-stop speed of our hectic lives creates a lot of jumbled thoughts, confusion, and noise inside our brains. It's a stressful existence that not many stop to consider – until, of course, that stress builds up and expresses itself in ways that cannot be ignored. Examples of physical ailments attributed to stress can be but are not limited to: fatigue, chronic pain, panic attacks, sore eyes and blurry vision, indigestion and heartburn. Stress is also associated heavily with a low quality of life and chronic unhappiness. One could (and should) ask, *What is the point of all the hustle and bustle if in the end it just makes you stressed out?*

Meditation, it turns out, can be the remedy and a preventative measure in one. It is a practice that seeks to clear the mind of distractions and mental detritus through a variety of mental and physical techniques that trains the brain to use focus and objectivity to find clarity. It sheds the nonessential by helping the practitioner identify and concentrate on what is important. A seasoned mediator will move through life with calm, lucidity, and self-possession.

A BRIEF HISTORY OF MEDITATION

Meditation has no known date of origin, but anthropologists believe humans were purposefully engaging in meditative practices as far back as 5000 BCE (Ross, 2016, para. 4). Though it is commonly associated with Eastern religions today, it is believed that hunter-gatherer societies meditated, which suggests that the practice did not start out as a religious one. As human movement expanded over the Middle and Far East, meditation spread as well. The ancient Egyptians and the first great dynasties of China incorporated meditation into their religious and spiritual practices, and it of course has a long and storied history in Hindu and Buddhist societies.

Today, the most common forms of meditation are usually tributaries of a practice known as the Vipassana tradition, which began in India nearly three thousand years ago. Vipassana translates to English as "to see things as they really are." It's not surprising then, that the ambition of this kind of meditation is to achieve a non-judgemental understanding of the present moment. This requires a great awareness of and focus on the self and the immediate environment. In today's vernacular, this kind of meditation is called *mindful meditation*. Daily practice of mindful meditation is credited with a host of physical health benefits, including reduced blood pressure, less chronic pain, better sleep, headache relief and many others. Beyond the physical, mindful meditation can help with stress management, increased focus and drive, reduced feelings of negativity, and even a boost in creativity. Mindful meditation is also the most researched type of meditation in the world, with thousands of scholarly and scientific studies to back up the claims of its devotees.

MEDITATION PRACTICES FOR THE MODERN WORLD

When most people think of meditation, they likely think of a person sitting criss-cross-apple-sauce with their eyes closed, perched on a tufted pillow, listening to windchimes or the sound of rain as they chant *om*. While this is certainly a form of meditation (known as transcendental meditation) it is not the only kind, and many find its rigid and particular parameters can make it difficult to incorporate the practice into a modern life.

So, what to do if you can't sit and chant for thirty minutes, twice a day? Here are some examples of modern meditative techniques, some of which you may already do without even knowing you're a practitioner of meditation!

Yoga

Yoga might be an obvious one, due to its common ancestry with meditation. Yoga was first mentioned in the Reg Vida, a sacred Indian text from five thousand years ago – about the same timeline that anthropologists believe meditation first began. Today there are six branches of yoga that all have a different focus and different aspects of practice. Commonly, and especially in the West, yoga is seen as simply physical exercise, particularly with the advent of such practices as flow and pilates, which use yoga poses, weights, and movement to challenge the body's stability. However, according to Swami Sivananda, a revered practitioner and teacher who developed the Sivananda method, yoga is a practice primarily for the mind, and while it is outwardly expressed through the physical, "[yoga poses & movements] are the third and fourth steps towards meditation. Stabilized meditative postures and regulation of the breath help tremendously in calming the mind down" (Sivananda, n.d.).

If you've ever been to a yoga class, you know that regardless of the level of fitness, there is a great emphasis placed on breathing, the mind to muscle connection, and being deeply rooted to the spiritual self. As your body moves through different poses, yoga seeks to ground you in the present moment.

Yoga has been steadily increasing in popularity since the 1960's, and today you don't even have to sign up for a class to reap the benefits. There are thousands of yoga routines for free online, from all six branches, suited to every lifestyle, and tailored to help ease every ailment, both physical and mental. Next time you find yourself at the end of a long, stressful week, hop onto Youtube and search for a beginner yoga routine aimed at relaxation.

Journaling

Many people with hectic schedules love to practice a relatively easy form of meditation by keeping a journal. Regularly writing in a journal allows the practitioner to quiet the mind through physically writing down the thoughts that cause them trouble or stress. Many people who journal with regularity say that writing down their thoughts allows them the space to let negative thoughts go and the room to be circumspect about the level of impact they've allowed stress and negativity to have on their life.

Journaling also provides the space to prioritize thoughts and feelings without the judgment of others – a cornerstone of meditation. A neutral viewpoint allows the journalist to shed such feelings as shame, embarrassment, or resentment. Journaling is also a great way to keep a log of emotional triggers and instances of negative self-talk. This log will help the practitioner examine the impact of these triggers and lead them to finding better ways to control them.

Journaling also has the benefit of being easy to start. All you need is a notebook, a writing utensil, and a few minutes of quiet. If you'd like to try your hand at mindful journaling, try sitting down and just writing whatever pops into your head. Don't pay attention to or get distracted by the rules of grammar, syntax, and spelling – just write what comes into your head. If that is too open ended for you, try focusing on one of these prompts:

- What are three thoughts you had that challenged you today?

- What are three thoughts you had that made you happy today?

- What are three things you did today that made you feel productive?

- What are three urges you had today that you resisted successfully?

Going Outside

This one might seem a little too rudimentary, but hear us out.

The health benefits of going outside cannot be ignored or denied. Adding a meditative approach to being outdoors can only add to the positive impact. The outside world is a world filled with different sights, sounds, and smells than even the best loved of our enclosed spaces. It evokes different feelings – feelings that human beings naturally and intuitively seek out. If we can take advantage of these unique stimuli, we can use them to turn our attention inward to further cultivate a quiet mind.

For example, next time you are outside, take a moment to pause, close your eyes, and pick out a single sound, perhaps the gentle rushing of the breeze through the trees. Allow this sound to ground you as you focus inward. Let your mind know only that sound and discard the other noises around you. Try to focus on how your mind responds to that sound. Does it feel peaceful? Relaxing? Does it fill you with happiness or a sense of purpose? If it doesn't, next time try to pick a sound that you instinctively think will. Sounds are powerful touchstones in our lives and have the ability to help us achieve clarity.

So now we know what meditation is, where it came from, and why humans like it so much. Now you may be asking yourself, How does meditation help with ADHD symptoms? And how do we know for sure that it's beneficial? In chapter three we will look at meditation as a way to manage ADHD and the scientific studies that prove it works.

Chapter 3
The Science Behind Meditation &
ADHD

While it seems perhaps counter-intuitive that our brain, an organ that exhibits behaviors and control over the body via a series of chemical reactions and electrical currents, could benefit from, essentially, just chilling the freak out, research tells us this is true. Western scientific inquiry first became interested in studying meditation in the 1960's, and since then there have been thousands of peer reviewed works published on the very real influence that meditation has over the brain.

In more recent decades, researchers have turned their attention to studying the effect that meditation has on the ADHD brain. As we know from chapter one, the ADHD brain is at a disadvantage due to low levels of neurotransmitters that facilitate communication within the different areas of the mind. The question is, *Can meditation still "brain train," even if the mechanisms that control memory, focus, and impulsivity are underdeveloped and under communicated?* The resounding and scientific answer is yes.

MEDITATION'S EFFECT ON ATTENTION

For decades, researchers have found a direct correlation between *increased cognition* and a stronger memory with better focus. Increased cognition is simply defined as the mind's ability to absorb knowledge. It was

19

not until 2013, however, that scientists at Oxford University developed a method to use medical imaging technology to accurately document physiological changes that occur in the brain due to consistent meditative practice. The results were remarkable!

According to the study, which was published in the journal of *Social Cognitive and Affective Neuroscience*, "Meditators, compared with controls, showed significantly greater cortical thickness in the [...] brain" and that "evidence suggests meditation alters the functional and structural plasticity of distributed neural processes underlying attention and emotion" (Kang, 2013). In layman's terms, meditating was found to actually and measurably increase the thickness of gray matter in the brain.

What is gray matter? Gray matter is a type of tissue specific to your brain and spinal cord that is filled with nerve cells, or neurons. Neurons are made up of three main components that are vital for inter brain communication:

1) A cell body with a nucleus that contains genetic material and controls cellular activity.

2) An axon that sends electrical signals within the brain and throughout the body.

3) Dendrites branches that receive signals from other cells.

The neurons that make up the brain's gray matter begin to develop in utero and continue to develop until about age eight. Gray matter continues to grow in density until about the age of twenty-two – the age by which developmental disorders present in an individual. Dense, or thick, gray matter is associated with high levels of brain processing, which allows for further mental development. Put simply, healthy gray matter is essential for receiving, understanding, and processing all information and stimuli.

Gray matter is particularly associated with the frontal cortex, an area of the brain that we already learned is deeply affected by ADHD and controls the mental skills that make up executive function. A thickening of this region can be likened to lifting weights to grow the muscles and become stronger. Clinically, thickened gray matter has shown to increase cognition, improving attention regulation and executive function for someone with ADHD.

MEDITATION & IMPULSE CONTROL

One of the more frustrating symptoms of ADHD is a lack of impulse control. The unpredictable and oftentimes rash behavior commonly associated with poor impulse control can lead to harsh consequences in all areas of life. People with ADHD are more likely to report strained and combative personal relationships, difficulty behaving appropriately in a professional setting, and feeling helpless to make the necessary changes in order to see improvements. In this way, the disorder becomes a burden that can have horrific consequences. A 2017 article published in the World Journal of Psychiatry that reviewed twenty-six studies on suicide and found that adults with ADHD experience suicide ideation twice as much as control groups without ADHD, and between 1.5 and 2.5 times more likely to attempt or complete suicide.

Obviously, these numbers are extremely upsetting, and as pharmaceuticals have little effect on emotional regulation, an alternative method of care is needed. If meditation is to be considered as an appropriate and effective remedy, it is paramount that its effect on impulsivity be empirically observable.

In order to prove this, researchers at the University of Wisconsin - Madison decided to expand upon the Oxford team's findings. They used imaging technology to not only physically map the structural differences as the Oxford team had done before them, but also to observe how strong the connections between parts of the brain became and how communications changed, if at all.

Again, the findings were incredible.

During the eight week study, a group of 1,105 participants with ADHD were either enrolled in a mindful meditation course, or were part of a control group that practiced no meditation at all. Their brains were image mapped at the beginning of the study and again once it had concluded. At the end of the study, brain mapping imagery found that an area of the brain we have briefly discussed before, called the amygdala, had structurally changed.

The amygdala is a structure deep within the temporal lobe at the center of the brain. It is often referred to as "primal" because it is essential to survival. It is responsible for raw emotional output, especially pain and anger, and where we instinctively sense danger, controlling our "fight, flight, or freeze" responses. It also connects our emotions to many other brain functions, such as the construction of memories. In the case of people with ADHD, the amygdala is shown to have atypical connections and abnormal interactions with the frontal cortex and basal ganglia, affecting how these two regions communicate to each other. In simpler terms, the amygdala is overactive, while the front cortex and the basal ganglia are under-active. This disruption adversely and chronically affects behavior and impulse control.

In the University of Wisconsin study, the group of participants who practiced mindful meditation all exhibited amygdalae that had shrunk following the eight weeks of the study. And, just like the scientists at Oxford had observed, the brain's gray matter had thickened. What is perhaps most interesting is that the previously abnormal connections also changed. Essentially, the amygdala exerted less control over the brain, while the frontal cortex and basal ganglia exerted more – proving definitively that meditation can increase a person's impulse control (Plessen, 2006), (Ireland, 2014).

MEDITATION & EMOTIONAL REGULATION

One area of particular interest to researchers studying the effects of meditation and ADHD symptoms management is that of emotional regulation. This is because pharmaceutical medications, whether stimulants or non-stimulants, do not address emotional regulation. While there is some research that suggests medication can nominally help the ADHD mind regulate emotions, for the most part, it is the one area that medicated people with ADHD see little to no improvement. This is thought to be because medication does not increase dopamine production.

Dopamine is of course one of the neurotransmitters that is in short supply in the ADHD brain. Dopamine is also the neurotransmitter responsible for communicating signals that carry emotional responses to different parts of the brain. It is known as the "happy hormone" because it is switched on during pleasurable experiences (Charron, 2022, para. 2).

Meditation is a calming, oftentimes pleasurable experience. It is no surprise then that researchers have found that meditation can increase the body's dopamine production by as much as 65% (Kajer, 2002). An increase in dopamine production has a strong connection to a person's ability to regulate their emotions. In the case of ADHD symptom management, however, meditation's effect on emotional regulation is twofold. We will discuss the second way it helps regulate emotions in chapter four.

MEDITATION & ADHD: WHAT THE DATA SAYS

While the results from the Oxford University and University of Wisconsin studies are fascinating, if you live with ADHD day in and day out, you are likely far more interested to know if the physiological findings have any bearing in the real world. What good is a smaller amygdala or thicker gray matter if your life is still being detrimentally impacted by a developmental disorder over which you have no control?

When it comes to studying the observable behavioral changes attributed to meditation in people with ADHD, the data is incredibly supportive. Particularly in children, newer research shows that mindful meditation helped improve cognitive function and emotional well being. After just ten minutes of instruction in mindful meditation, children are able to demonstrate an increase in working memory and impulse control and are also able to switch tasks more smoothly. Additionally, the short meditation sessions help children control their emotional responses as well as provide a mood boost (Bigalow, 2021).

Parents also find that their ADHD children benefit greatly from meditation, with many reporting that their kids are less hyperactive, more calm, and better able to express themselves (Santonastaso, et al., 2020).

It's not only children who find they like the effects of meditation. A review of thirty-one scholarly studies show meditation to be far more effective for managing ADHD symptoms in adults than life skills training and education. Adults with ADHD who keep to a daily practice of meditation anywhere from five to fifteen minutes long, find they are better able to stay focused on tasks. They also find that the comorbidities often associated with ADHD (namely depression and anxiety) lessened dramatically (Levine, et al., 2018).

While no one is suggesting that meditation will ever or should ever take the place of medication, the facts cannot be denied. Incorporating a regular meditation routine as an adjunct to pharmaceutical treatment greatly improves the most common and frustrating symptoms associated with ADHD. As such, it also drastically improves the quality of life for people who have been struggling with the effects of the disorder.

Chapter 4
Types of Meditation Practices for
ADHD

W hile progress is made every day, there is still so much we do not know or understand about the brain. The singularity of brain chemistry means that Just as medication is not a one size fits all for ADHD, the meditative techniques that will work for one person, may not work for another. The process of cultivating a practice that works for you will require patience and oftentimes trial and error.

We will spend this chapter going over some of the more common meditation practices for those with attention deficit/hyperactivity disorder, as well as who might best benefit from them. This should not be considered an exhaustive list, however. One might find the best results with something not included here, or even with a combination of these and other meditative practices.

MINDFULNESS

In previous chapters we have used the phrase *mindful meditation*. To understand what makes mindful meditation unique, we will first come up with a working definition of the term mindfulness.

Mindfulness is the act of present moment awareness. This may seem like an unneeded and redundant distinction to make; after all, are we not always aware of the present moment? But take a moment to think and ask yourself these questions: How much of my worries stem from the unknowable future? How much of my anger and pain are products of my past? Mindfulness tasks us with shedding these hindrances in order to be grounded in immediacy. It asks us to observe ourselves as we are, right now.

Also key to practicing mindfulness is, once we are grounded in the present moment, to observe our thoughts and emotions without trying to interpret them or assign value. Mindfulness then is ***the practice of being a passive, non-judgemental observer to our own being in order to see ourselves as we are***.

This tends to differ from other forms of meditation, which seeks an "awareness of Nothing". Transcendental meditation, for example, requires the practitioner to meditate for a specific, extended period of time and attempt to reach a state of clarity through emptying the mind of all thoughts and emotions. Mindfulness, in contrast, can be practiced anywhere at any time, and urges the practitioner to reach a state of calmness through the awareness of Something – Something being yourself in the present moment.

The process of practicing mindful meditation is fairly straightforward. Once the mind becomes accustomed to turning inward, you'll find that you can do so at any time, in any setting, without any disruption to your usual routines. In the beginning, though, it will be helpful to follow the following steps.

Schedule a dedicated time to practice.

This is particularly important for those with ADHD as, generally speaking, the ADHD mind is not used to prolonged periods of intense focus. Pick a time when you will not be distracted by the stressors or responsibilities of daily life, and start with just a minute or two. You will likely find that ideal times are either when you are first waking up in the morning or just before you are getting into bed at night, but it doesn't have to be. The true ideal time for you will be when you are most likely to sit and meditate.

Observe the present moment.

Situate yourself so that you are able to sit or stand quietly and comfortably. Close your eyes, and let the present moment come to you in fragments before you try to grasp the whole. What's the temperature of the environment where you are? What can you hear? What do you smell? Focus on your breath in and out of your lungs and let yourself relax.

It's important to remember the ambition of mindfulness, which is to exist without judgment in the present moment. Deep meditation or an empty mind are not the goals here. Sit quietly with your eyes closed and don't think about the day you've had or the day to come. Just be where you are.

Accept and release thoughts or judgment.

Inevitably, especially at the start of your mindfulness journey, your mind will stray to any number of topics: work you have to complete, an argument you had earlier, a phone call you have to return, even what you're going to have for dinner later. This makes sense, because the brain has been trained to think and worry constantly. It is through a dedicated mindfulness practice that you will train it to think differently. When a stray thought finds its way into the forefront of your mind during your practice, simply acknowledge it and let it pass.

It's also inevitable that you will find yourself trying to interpret these thoughts, or even pass judgment on them. When this happens, repeat the above: observe and allow the judgment to drift away. By not lingering on it, it loses its power.

In addition to the above principles, there are four easy to follow steps when transitioning your mindful meditation journey into your everyday life.. They can be easily followed by remembering the acronym STOP and are most helpful when you find yourself in instances of heightened emotional dysregulation:

Stop yourself in the middle of whatever you are doing or saying and give yourself a moment. Remember, there is *always* time to delay harmful behavior.

Take a breath. Practice a moment of focused breathing and let yourself be in the moment. Count your breath into the count of four and out to the count of four. Do this as many times as you need to get grounded in the present.

Observe and acknowledge your negative feelings. Do not judge yourself or slide into a guilt spiral. Simply acknowledge them and gently allow yourself to move on.

Proceed. Now that you have grounded yourself in the present moment, you can continue with what you were doing.

Mindful meditation is the most researched form of meditation, with decades of scientific review and thousands of studies to back up its effectiveness. In recent years it has become incredibly popular with people who have ADHD because the practice of mindful meditation uses the steps above to train the brain to be self-aware. This can help identify specific triggers that induce ADHD symptoms. Many ADHD practitioners find that their impulsivity and emotional dysregulation decrease with mindful meditation.

GUIDED VISUALIZATION

Another popular form of meditation for those with ADHD is the *guided visualization* technique. This technique most generally involves listening to a recording or a guide that is meant to help you navigate your practice. It is commonly used by psychologists in therapies for patients with high levels of stress and anxiety. However, it can easily be self-taught and practiced alone.

The concept is simple: in a quiet space the practitioner visualizes a calm scene or image. The aim is to spend time with the scene and to use all five senses to stay grounded in it. The scene can be something as simple as laying on the banks of a river and watching the water move peacefully downstream. Or, it can be as involved and specific as visualizing white blood cells ridding the body of disease.

If you think guided visualization sounds like a technique that could work for you, start small, as you would with mindful meditation. Something wonderful and very beginner friendly about this technique is that there are many guided visualizations for free online. A quick Google or Youtube search for "guided visualization for beginners" will yield literally thousands of results. There are also a number of popular apps that specialize in this technique, such as Calm, Headspace, and Buddhify. Many of them, though, cost money for a subscription, so be sure to do your research before agreeing to any terms.

Those with ADHD tend to like guided visualization, as the short attention span associated with the disorder can make other forms of meditation difficult. Guided visualization gives the ADHD practitioner a specific image to focus on so the mind doesn't wander. When adopted as a regular practice, guided visualization has been proven to lower stress, increase emotional regulation, and help focus. It's also been used to successfully lower blood pressure, quit smoking, and help with sleep disorders.

LOVING-KINDNESS MEDITATION

A *loving-kindness meditation* is one that specifically aims to cultivate compassion for others and oneself. Rather than focusing on the present moment, however, loving-kindness meditation seeks to sow compassion in an enduring way, for now and into the future. In this way, it is deeply rooted in Buddhist spiritual philosophy and many who practice loving-kindness meditation follow the teachings of Buddha, though doing so is not at all a requirement.

In order to develop compassion, the practice involves repeating phrases, either to yourself or out loud, that direct kindness and love toward yourself and others in a total of five stages. The five stages to a loving-kindness meditation are:

- Loving Kindness for Yourself
- Loving Kindness for a Good Friend

- Loving Kindness for a Neutral Person

- Loving Kindness for a Difficult Person

- Loving Kindness for All Sentient Beings.

The repeated phrases may differ and can be tailored to your preferences, but in general the script needs to be repeated for all five stages, and for a set amount of time for each. A sample script that is quite common within the practice is:

Loving Kindness for Yourself: *May I be happy. May I be healthy. May I be safe. May I live with ease.*

As you repeat this meditation to yourself, for however long you choose, picture yourself living happily, healthy, safe and with ease.

Loving Kindness for a Good Friend: *May you be happy. May you be healthy. May you be safe. May you live with ease.*

As you repeat this meditation, picture your friend living happily, healthy, safe, and with ease.

Loving Kindness for a Neutral Person: *May you be happy. May you be healthy. May you be safe. May you live with ease.*

As you repeat this meditation, picture now this person living happily, healthy, safe, and with ease.

Loving Kindness for a Difficult Person: *May you be happy. May you be healthy. May you be safe. May you live with ease.*

As you repeat this meditation, picture now this person living happily, healthy, safe, and with ease.

Loving Kindness for All Sentient Beings: *May we be happy. May we be healthy. May we be safe. May we live with ease.*

As you repeat this meditation, picture all life in the universe living in harmony: happy, healthy, safe, and with ease.

You may find it more difficult to draw pictures in your mind and cultivate compassion as your level of intimacy with the person you are directing the loving kindness to decreases. Maybe you feel you actively dislike the person and so it's very difficult for you. That's okay, and even to be expected. Cultivating compassion is learned through practice and repetition, very similar to how mindful meditation and guided visualization train the brain to regulate emotions and attention.

Loving-kindness meditation is growing more popular with people with ADHD because those with the disorder are more likely to have lower self-esteem and less self-confidence when compared to their neurotypical peers. As we've learned, that low opinion of self can lead to clinical depression and other comorbidities. A loving-kindness meditation practice can help combat the negative self-talk that people with ADHD tend to exhibit, and either curb or prevent depressive episodes.

MOVEMENT-BASED MEDITATION

As discussed in chapter two, yoga is a type of meditative technique, though it is not the only movement based meditation practice there is. Almost any form of movement can be meditative if done with intention and awareness of the body, the self in the body, and the sensations that occur within and to the body during movement. Yoga is popular, but Tai Chi, dancing, swimming, walking – all can be considered forms of meditative movement.

Movement based meditation is popular with children who have ADHD. The meditative aspect teaches them bodily awareness, which helps with hyperactivity and fidgeting. Movement is also a great way to boost dopamine production and is generally more novice-friendly than other forms of meditation.

Now that we have a solid knowledge base in meditation and understand the benefits it has on ADHD symptom management, we can begin establishing our practice. The next chapters will serve as a guide to setting yourself up for success when starting your meditation journey.

Chapter 5
Getting Started with Meditation

L ike most things in life, starting a successful meditation practice requires a little bit of forethought and effort. While anyone can learn and benefit from meditation, it is of particular importance to people with ADHD that the environment and routine be established early and maintained so that when challenges and obstacles arise (as they are guaranteed to do), there is a solid foundation to fall back on and reactionary responses or negativity won't derail progress entirely.

First thing being first, we will talk about the physical space in which to meditate.

CREATING A SUPPORTIVE MEDITATION SPACE

When setting up a meditation area or room, it's essential that it exude *calmness*. While calm has variable and relative definitions, it's generally agreed upon that the space should be quiet and have only positive associations for you. Try to avoid areas in which you work or tend to life's daily duties. Places such as a home office or a living room where children frequently play and leave toys are not great areas to meditate in, as it is more likely the mind will wander to work or tidying, etc.

Be sure to keep your space *clean and free of clutter*. Clutter has a habit of following us into the mind and scattering our thoughts. Plus, clean spaces are just more serene to be in. The more tranquil you feel in your meditation space, the more likely you'll be to spend time there and the better your practice will be.

Next, make it ***comfortable***. Wear loose fitting clothes in natural fabrics as a best practice; clothes that fit tight against the body are more restrictive and thus distracting. You can also add elements to the space that prioritize your comfort. Things like a meditation cushion or mat in colors you love or fabrics you like will make daily practice more enjoyable. These things are not required, though, and if you find yourself perfectly comfortable sitting on the floor, that's perfectly fine.

When it comes to lighting your space, ***natural light*** is always better than harsh ambient lighting. If you find that you like to meditate either very early in the morning or at night when it's dark, add task lighting in the form of a floor or table lamp with a warm bulb. (Generally speaking, you don't want to go above 3000 Kelvin, and minimal brightness of preferably around 500 lumens.) Bright lights, cool toned lights, and overhead lighting are much more stimulating, and will make it difficult for you to reach a fully meditative state.

If you can, bring the outdoors in with some ***potted plants***. According to a study in *Perspectives on Psychological Science,* olfaction (sense of smell) is directly linked to emotional centers in the brain and are tied to a plethora of brain functions, such as making memories and emotional regulation (Manzani et al, 2021). There are many plants that have very fragrant bouquets that can help you relax. Chamomile, sage, eucalyptus, and bergamot are all commonly used in aromatherapy to promote relaxation. Lavender is the most studied scent for aiding relaxation and is believed to interact strongly with the amygdala and limbic system as a whole (Ghavami et al, 2022).

Not everyone has a green thumb, which is perfectly fine. Consider bringing in a vase and some fresh grocery store flowers, or using a diffuser.

An ***essential oil diffuser*** mixes drops of fragrant oils with water and mist them continuously into the air, effectively perfuming the room. Depending on how big your meditation area is, a small, inexpensive diffuser will be enough to cover the entire space. There are many different combinations of oils that promote calmness and relaxation, or you can even get creative and make your own blends using your favorite smells. Some tried and true fusions are: basil, bergamot, grapefruit, and lemon oils for clarity; frankincense, sage, and Palo Santo oils for tranquility; and sandalwood, cedarwood, and cistus for relaxation.

If you find you are highly sensitive to smells and having them in your space is distracting, don't use them.

Finally, ***personalize your space***. No matter what meditation technique you choose to use, your practice is going to be deeply personal to you. It follows then that so should be your meditation space. Decorate the area with personal photos and mementos that evoke positive, happy emotions in you. Items such as cards, trinkets, favorite books, or beloved souvenirs can all have a place and a role in supporting your meditation practice.

Of course, you may find that you are perfectly happy sitting in a quiet park with no pillow, diffuser, or mementos. And that's perfectly fine! There is no correct or mandatory way to set up a meditation space. The only necessary component is that it is a space you love. Think of it this way: the lovelier your space feels to you, the more time you'll want to spend there.

ESTABLISHING A REGULAR MEDITATION ROUTINE

It can be daunting to dive into a meditation routine as a novice. Keep these four tips in mind as you begin your journey.

1. Start small.

Studies on meditation and people with ADHD found the most success with meditation when they started out meditating for one to three minutes at a time, twice a day. Gradually, over a period of weeks, the time was increased to ten to fifteen minutes (Kelly, 2022).

2. Try using music as a grounding guide.

Nowhere does it say you must meditate in silence, and many people find sound to be very grounding. If you subscribe to a music streaming service, there are many playlists curated specifically for meditation, but you don't have to use them. If you prefer to put together your own playlist, try putting on a mellow, mid tempo song, preferably without any vocals. Time your breaths to the beat of the song and focus on the steadiness of your inhales and exhales. The rhythm will help you reach a deep and meditative state.

Eventually, you'll try meditating without music, as heavily relying on music can interfere with practicing mindfulness in your daily life. Imagine that you need to take a moment to ground yourself at work or in class and you can't because you don't have the correct playlist. It's important to train the brain to easily and readily slip into a nonjudgmental present, but using music in the beginning is perfectly fine and can be very helpful.

3. Pick a time to meditate and stick to it.

Let's make something very clear: it doesn't matter what time of day you meditate, so long as you do. But, are you more likely to stick to a routine if you meditate at the same time(s) every day? Absolutely. Especially when you are first establishing your practice, the repetitiveness of a set routine will help you form the habit. Try to choose a time that you know you are less likely to be stressed out or anxious, such as in the morning when you first wake up, and/or at night before you fall asleep.

4. Expand your practice… eventually.

Meditation is a tool, so it stands to reason that it can and should be used during times when it will benefit you in the moment, such as instances of heightened emotional duress. Especially for people with ADHD, learning to turn to mindfulness during stressful, frustrating, or triggering moments, or instances when symptoms feel unbearable, is key to managing the disorder. After you have built a routine, expand it so that when your ADHD symptoms feel as though they are in the driver's seat, you can calmly retake control by using the STOP process discussed in the previous chapter.

OVERCOMING CHALLENGES & OBSTACLE

It's an objective and observable fact of life that setbacks will happen. They are inescapable and affect everyone without prejudice. It may surprise you to learn that even when it comes to mindful meditation, there are challenges that every practitioner encounters. Don't let these obstacles convince you to abandon your practice altogether. A better mindset to have is to approach the setback itself from a mindfulness perspective. That is to say, nonjudgmentally and with compassion for yourself.

Here we have laid out five common challenges that even a person who is the most dedicated to and adept at meditation will face, often many times over, throughout the life of their practice. In addition, we offer insight into how to overcome them so that when you face them down the road, you will be prepared to tackle them with confidence.

Obstacle: *The fear that it won't work.*

At the beginning of your meditation practice, you may find that you feel a lot of doubt; doubt that the practice will work, doubt that you will be good at it, doubt over the future, etc. Doubt is a natural emotion to have, but if we take a closer look at the nature of doubt we'll find that oftentimes the underlying emotion is fear. People have a tendency to let the fear of failure limit them. The logic seems to be that if you never try, then you can't fail. However, the reverse is also true: if you never try, you can't succeed.

How to overcome: Allow thoughts and emotions to be simply thoughts and emotions, not facts. Just because you are afraid meditation won't work doesn't mean it won't actually work. Acknowledge the fear without judgment, accept that there are things you cannot know, and then let it go and continue with your practice.

Obstacle: *Feeling restless.*

Restlessness is a very common challenge for people new to meditation, and particularly those with ADHD. If you are unused to being still or intentionally reflective, it may take a while for you to fully relax and reach a meditative state.

How to overcome: Consider trying a movement based meditation technique, like yoga or Tai Chi. Listening to your body and acknowledging the restlessness in a non judgemental way will help you practice mindfulness, while choosing a meditative movement will still allow you to develop your meditation routine.

Obstacle: *Feeling drowsy.*

Another very common challenge, drowsiness, can sneak up on you when meditating. Sometimes your body and mind become so relaxed that you will start to fall asleep. This is completely normal and does not mean that you are bad at meditating or that meditating will not work for you. It simply means that you're tired.

How to overcome: As a form of trouble-shooting, try adjusting your posture to a more upright position, with your shoulders square and your spine in a neutral, comfortable position. Do not elevate your chin, but also don't let it droop downward toward your chest. If you find that drowsiness persists while you meditate, try switching your routine to a pre-bedtime practice aimed at ensuring restful sleep.

Obstacle: *Feelings of frustration.*

Like doubt, feelings of frustration or irritation are completely natural and could arise in you for a variety of reasons, some having nothing at all to do with your meditation practice. Maybe something frustrated you earlier in the day or week, or perhaps you have a problem to solve and are irritated with yourself that you're stalled on the solution. Whatever the reason, take heart in the knowledge that negative emotions affect everyone and are part of the human experience.

How to overcome: There is a saying in mindfulness: *what we resist will persist.* When negative thoughts or emotions turn up in your mind, don't try to excuse, fight or deny them. Instead, let yourself be a detached observer who can look at the frustration, accept it, and let it leave. Getting into the habit of accepting frustration and moving on from it will eventually lead to mastering the feeling so that it can no longer cause a reactive response in you. This will further lead to you controlling your emotions, and not the other way around.

Obstacle: *The desire to stop meditating.*

There will be times in your practice where mindful meditation feels like a chore or a waste of time. You may even have a period of days or weeks where you find it extremely difficult to convince yourself to meditate. Again, this is normal and not an indication that meditation doesn't work for you or that you should quit your practice.

How to overcome: Be compassionate with yourself, but also remind yourself that there have been and will be many times in life where you must do something you don't particularly want to do simply because it's good for you. A regular mindful meditation practice provides a massive return on investment for the relatively small amount of time you need to devote to it each day. Let yourself feel however you find you need to feel about meditation in the moment, and then turn back to your practice.

There are obviously more obstacles and setbacks that can and likely will arise, but hopefully these examples have helped to steer you toward the tools needed to move past them efficiently and quickly.

As you get deeper into your practice and build confidence with meditation, you will find that many of the tools and strategies used during meditation can be transposed into other areas of your life. This is particularly true for those most affected by an ADHD diagnosis. In the next chapter, we will discuss mindfulness tactics to help self-awareness and emotional regulation that can be used at any time.

Chapter 6
Mindfulness Strategies for Everyday Life

A s has been discussed in previous chapters, ADHD is a disorder that has the ability to affect every area of a person's life. While medication can and should be discussed with a physician, there is a wealth of scientific research and data that supports meditation as a supplemental therapy. While a regular meditation routine is essential to training the brain in areas of cognitive function affected by ADHD, symptoms of the disorder can and will spring up unannounced. What becomes incumbent upon the practitioner then, is finding ways to introduce mindfulness techniques into their everyday life, not just during a controlled meditation session.

MINDFULNESS TECHNIQUES FOR IMPULSIVITY & REACTIVITY

What is reactivity? If we define it using a mindfulness lens, it is "reacting out of our habitual patterns without consciousness" (Brach, n.d.). Reading this definition, what two words stand out to you?

Patterns and *consciousness*.

Mindfulness does two things. First, when practiced consistently, it trains the brain through repetition to adopt new and more healthy *patterns*. Trained behaviors stimulate the reward centers in the brain, which in turn increase dopamine production. Increased dopamine production increases the efficiency and efficacy of the limbic system, which we know from chapter two regulates our emotions. In this way, mindful meditation has a direct, physiological impact on impulsiveness and reactivity.

But mindfulness also affects the *consciousness*. The mind of a person practicing mindful meditation learns, again through repetition, to self-reflect and hold compassion for themselves. As we've said many times, observing thoughts and emotions without judgment allows acceptance and control over emotions.

Perhaps an example will be helpful here. Imagine you are busy running errands on a day when you have a long to-do list and your schedule is packed and tight. You go to the grocery store for a few items and leave to take them to your car. Once you get there, you notice that someone has hit your car with their vehicle and left without leaving a note. This makes you both frustrated and angry, maybe you are even shocked. You impulsively curse out loud. As you're trying to get a closer look at the damage, your grocery bag breaks and the contents tumble onto the ground, breaking eggs and spilling milk, etc. This only further heightens your anger and frustration. You react to those feelings by kicking your car, which causes you to break your toe, which necessitates a trip to the doctors and derails your entire day.

This is maybe an extreme example, but it shows us two things. First, oftentimes negativity begets negativity. If you allow negative emotions to control you, you are likely to cause a chain reaction of more negative emotions. Second, reactive behavior hurts ourselves and never yields the results we want.

Now let's flip the script, using the same example. You get to your car, groceries in hand to find the scrapes and dents left by another driver. You start to feel the anger, frustration, and disbelief rise within you. Instead of letting those emotions steer the ship, you recognize the emotions for what they are: temporary. You pause and take a few deep breaths. You let yourself observe the anger and frustration as though from a distance, passively observing without judging yourself or the person who hit your car. Instead, you simply acknowledge that you are angry and frustrated and let the feelings pass. You continue to breathe. You direct your senses to the world around you as it is in the current moment; the warmth of the sun, the sounds of the parking lots, the smells. Once you are grounded, you open your eyes and you calmer and present in the moment, not struggling to navigate emotional triggers. You open the trunk, put the groceries inside, and continue on with your day. The damage to your car will be taken care of. That is, after all, what insurance is for.

As the above illustrates, mindfulness doesn't stop anger or frustration altogether. Instead, it allows you to own those feelings, rather than letting those feelings own you. Not only does pausing to ground yourself stop a chain reaction of negativity, but it also ensures that the day is not lost to those feelings. The more this technique is practiced, the easier it is to be present in the moment and the less those initial feelings will arise.

MINDFULNESS TECHNIQUES TO IMPROVE ATTENTION & TASK COMPLETION

One thing that a practitioner of mindful meditation is sure to become an expert in, is focus. That statement may seem hyperbolic to someone who struggles with executive dysfunction and attention dysregulation, which are two of the most reported and most exhausting symptoms of ADHD. Luckily, mindfulness can be practiced while doing a variety of everyday activities. Focusing on smaller, seemingly inconsequential things will train your brain to focus on larger things, as well as follow through with important tasks. Below are some examples of simple mindful meditation practices that will improve focus.

- **People watching.** While out and about, pick out a person and observe them. Make note of their body language, gestures, gait if they're walking, their posture if not. Try to observe how their body takes up space in the world. If you can hear them speak, note their tone of voice. Notice their appearance; what kinds of clothes are they wearing? Do they look comfortable? People watching will teach your mind to pay attention to detail as well as appreciate that detail is always a part of a whole. Think of it as learning to toggle between a micro and macro view, a skill that will help with multitasking and working memory. Remember, though, you are observing without judgment or any attempt to interpret what you are seeing.

- **Focused breathing.** We have discussed this one briefly in previous chapters, but it is worth it to go into further detail here. Sit or stand in an upright and comfortable position with an unforced and neutral spine. Take a breath and count to four as you inhale, and to four again as you exhale. As you breathe, try to imagine the mechanisms of your body that are working. Picture your lungs expanding as you take in air. Picture your diaphragm working to support your lungs. Take the time to really think about and picture the oxygen molecules attaching themselves to your red blood cells and being taken through the chambers of your heart and distributed throughout your body. As you picture these things, try to feel them happening. This kind of deep and intense focus will help with attention regulation, a key function of the frontal cortex.

- **Body check.** Somewhat similar to focused breathing, the body check (also called a body scan) is a form of mindfulness that requires taking a minute during the day to really tune into your body. Start at the top of your head or the tips of your toes and travel the length of your body slowly, noticing every body part, joint, muscle, and bone. As you do this, let yourself become aware of every strain and ache, every single point of tension, every part that feels tired or hurts. As you find them, don't try to adjust or relieve any discomfort; just observe and move on. This exercise in particular is a great alternative to looking at your phone when you find yourself with spare moments throughout the day, maybe while waiting in line or sitting in traffic.

- **Meditative chores.** Pick a daily chore that you are responsible for and make it one that you normally dislike doing. Visualize how you want the process to feel and what you want the outcome to be. Further visualize how you will feel once you finish the goal and achieve your desired outcome. As you begin actually doing the chore, focus on every detail. Pay attention to the process and make note of things that can be improved upon. The next day, make the adjustments and repeat the same meditation.

These exercises are easy to do and do not require you to sequester yourself away in order to do them. You will notice that as you practice and dedicate yourself to intense focus through these exercises, that the ability to focus will carry over into other areas of your life, such as work or school.

MINDFULNESS TECHNIQUES TO IMPROVE SLEEP

Before we get into how to combat sleep issues, let's first understand what disruptive sleeping is and its consequences.

Disordered sleeping is very common for those with attention deficit/hyperactivity disorder as ADHD is known to disrupt the natural circadian rhythms of the body. A circadian rhythm are changes that occur physically, environmentally, and behaviorally within the twenty-four hour span of a day that let the body know when it is time to sleep (Pacheco & Pacheco, 2023). For example, the day going from sunlight to the darkness of light, or how your body seems to become more tired the moment you get into bed, or how you seem to get more drowsy after an evening shower.

A disruption in this rhythm, whether caused by ADHD or not, upsets the sleep cycle, which is a necessary physiological cycle that happens in four stages in ninety minute increments repeatedly throughout a long period of sleep (generally six to eight hours). These stages include rapid eye movement (REM), and non-rapid eye movement

(NREM), which is further broken down into three stages, N1, N2, and N3. N3 is the deepest stage of sleep and believed to be the most restorative and therefore essential for the body (Patel, 2022). If the inability to reach N3 in the sleep cycle becomes chronic, it can result in: shortened attention span, poor judgment, reduced awareness of the environment and situation, reduced decision-making skills, poorer memory and reduced concentration (DHHS, n.d.).

You'll notice that all of these are already symptoms of ADHD. We can conclude then that ADHD can cause sleep disorders, which will exacerbate the already detrimental symptoms of ADHD.

Pharmaceuticals are another factor to consider when assessing sleep issues. Those who take stimulants to treat ADHD may find that their medications make it difficult to fall asleep and stay asleep. Whatever the reason, the connection between sleep disorders and ADHD is very real. Fortunately, the connection between mindful meditation and restful sleep is also very real.

Practicing mindfulness by being attune to your body and when it naturally starts to become fatigued will help guide your best sleep practices. You can start by setting up a sleep area that promotes good and restful sleep. First, establish a rule that the bed is only for sleeping; no eating, watching screens, or reading in bed. Next, make sure that the room is dark and cool. According to a Harvard Medicine study, the body's core temperature drops by one or two degrees while sleeping in order to conserve energy. You can achieve sleep faster by lowering the temperature in the room and helping this process along (Djik & Czeisler, 1995). After achieving the optimal temperature (somewhere between 60° and 65°), next make sure that the room is neither too quiet nor too loud. If either the quiet or background noises disturb you, consider a white noise machine.

After your sleep environment is set up, establish a bedtime routine and make sure it is the exact same every night. Yep, you are once again going to train your brain through repetition. Pick a "lights out" time and about an hour before, avoid looking at screens as much as possible. There is considerable new evidence that suggests the blue light emitted from phone, tablet, and television screens can adversely affect the circadian rhythm (CDC, n.d.). Once lights out time hits, go to bed.

It's important to be discerning about physical activities just before bedtime, as intense exercise can release endorphins, which may make it difficult to fall asleep. This makes bedtime the perfect time to practice mindful meditation.

If you need to move your body, find a gentle and relaxing yoga routine, but generally speaking the best mindfulness practices that promote sleep are mindful meditation and guided meditation. Meditation gently guides you to calmness and relaxation, which are the natural states the mind and body seek out in order to fall asleep and stay asleep. A regular meditation and bedtime routine will eventually lead you to falling asleep more quickly, staying asleep for longer periods of time, and sleeping more deeply – all of which will help manage ADHD symptoms.

Chapter 7
Building Emotional Resilience

WHAT IS STRESS?

It may seem surprising, but stress is actually a vital part of human life. Stress and anxiety are the emotional manifestation of normal chemical reactions in the brain that occur as a response to situations that we find challenging or threatening. Stress can be a good thing. In the ideal scenario, stress motivates us to solve problems and address challenges. Everyone will experience stress at some point in their lives, and to different degrees. It's a natural reaction and when well managed, can actually help cognitive function (World Health Organization, 2022).

What our human minds and evolution have not accounted for, however, is a modern world's exceedingly fast pace, addictive technological advances that can isolate us from our communities, and a hustle culture that eschews anything but constant work and advancement. Additionally, shared cultural stressors such as a global pandemic, mass shootings, and climate change can dogpile on more mental tension and anxiety.

It is no wonder, then, that 73% of American adults report suffering from the psychological symptoms of stress, which can include marked changes in appetite, fatigue, low sex drive, loneliness, irritability, or prolonged states of worry. 77% of American adults report showing the physical signs of stress as well, which can include rashes, headaches, panic attacks, constipation or diarrhea, high blood pressure, and chronic aches or pains. Women who experience the physical signs of stress can also report missed periods and other menstrual cycle related irregularities.

Both the psychological and physical reactions to stress can cause severe emotional responses, as well. People who suffer from chronic and/or acute stress consistently report poor and worsening mental health problems including major depressive disorder, obsessive compulsive disorder, and panic disorder. Alarmingly, those who experience high levels of stress are also at higher risk for substance abuse (Sinha, 2008).

STRESS & ADHD

Those with ADHD know that the symptoms associated with ADHD can themselves cause stress. Dr. Desiree Murray, an associate director of research at the Frank Porter Graham Child Development Institute at the University of North Carolina claims there is strong evidence that the relationship between ADHD and stress is bidirectional. This means that when symptoms of ADHD cause stress, that stress in turn makes the ADHD symptoms worse, causing more stress. It's the definition of a vicious cycle.

Stress's influence on the frontal cortex is very similar to the way ADHD affects the same area. In the case of stress, it's through a chemical reaction with the release of a hormone called cortisol, commonly called the "stress hormone". This reaction can lead to poor concentration, poor working memory, restlessness and fidgeting, and indecisiveness. If you have ADHD, particularly if you primarily have the inattentive presentation, then you are well aware that these are all symptoms of the disorder as well. Because of the relationship between ADHD and stress, these symptoms can become worse and heightened, resulting in chronic stress and severe ADHD.

There is also research that suggests stress exacerbates the emotional dysregulation common with ADHD. The effects, among other things, personal relationships. Stress can cause emotional withdrawal, leading to distraction and a lack of intimacy or affection. It can also cause impulsiveness and hyperactivity, which often results in impatience and careless communication – if you've ever said something you regretted to someone you cared about because you were stressed, then you know exactly what we're talking about. If you are already emotionally dysregulated due to ADHD, these symptoms will only get worse.

STRATEGIES TO MANAGE STRESS

Luckily there are many ways to help control the amount of stress in your life. Obviously, we are mostly concerned with a mindful and meditative approach, but in the interest of thoroughness, here is a brief list of some others:

- Take breaks from social media and news. Studies have shown that trying to keep up with the twenty-four hour news cycle is incredibly bad for stress and overall mental health.

- Prioritize sleep.

- Exercise regularly (even if it's just a walk around the block once a day), and eat a balanced diet.

- Make time for yourself and your hobbies.

- Connect with your friends, family, and community.

- Limit alcohol and caffeine consumption, both of which can spike cortisol levels.

MINDFUL MEDITATION & STRESS

Using our recently acquired knowledge about the well documented links between meditation and calmness, increased dopamine production, and reduced symptoms of ADHD, we can deduce that developing a regular meditation practice can dramatically alter the stress in our lives for the better.

Due to the wealth of literature that backs up this claim, mindful meditation when used to reduce stress actually has a clinical name: ***mindfulness-based stress reduction***, or MBSR. MBSR has very specific parameters when used as a therapeutic intervention, and is generally only used when someone has been diagnosed with chronic stress by a healthcare professional.

MBSR involves an eight week program that utilizes weekly, guided meditation in a group setting. It also teaches daily mindfulness exercises to be done at home. While the exact practices may vary from group to group, overall the success rate of MBSR is incredibly high, with an average of 75% of participants across multiple studies reporting significantly less stress and comorbidities associated with stress, like panic attacks and high blood pressure.

However, you do not need to be clinically diagnosed to feel the effects of stress, particularly if and when those effects are magnified by ADHD. And since it is fair to say that living with ADHD is in and of itself a stressful experience, it's helpful to have some mindful exercises at the ready to mitigate stress.

We know that mindfulness increases self-awareness by grounding the practitioner in the present moment. But when you're dealing with heightened levels of stress, it can be extremely difficult to get to a mindset in which you are fully and completely able to let go of anxieties, fears, and frustrations – all things that keep us from being entirely present. Rest assured that this is okay. In fact, you can begin your practice by acknowledging exactly that.

Try this simple visualization: Picture a deck of cards. It looks and feels like a normal deck except that on each card there is one thought or worry that has been troubling you. Picture yourself flipping through this deck slowly. As you flip through the deck, take note of the feelings that come up as you read the cards. How many of these feelings of anxiety and stress are due to an unknowable future? How many are to do with things that have happened in the past?

Now, picture – really picture, in as much detail as possible – yourself reading the cards again without any strong, emotional reaction. You are observing the cards as though it is just any old playing deck, and your attitude when you read your worries on the cards should look benign when you picture it.

Now, stack the deck and set them aside, face down. This is you acknowledging that you cannot control the future, and you cannot change the past. Release the negative emotions gently and with no judgment, and continue with your practice.

Once the deck is gone, let yourself come back into awareness of your body. Check in with your breathing, let your body move with expansion on every inhale and relax with every exhale. Notice your shoulders. Are they bunched up? Intentionally drop them and imagine that you can physically feel the tension fall off of you. Are your teeth clenched? Unstick your tongue from the roof of your mouth and relax your jaw. Picture more tension falling away. Finally, allow yourself to feel comforted by the fact that you exist in the present moment and the present moment has no use or room for stress.

This mindful meditation uses focus to accept our lack of control, which in turn causes us to give up any notion of perfectionism. It also crucially lists out triggers for us to learn from. If one of your cards says WORK, for example, then you can deduce that your work-life balance needs attention. Of course, cards may not be so general. Perhaps you're stressed out about flying somewhere for a trip and so one of your cards says PLANE CRASH or similar on it. You can take note of that and practice further by taking the time to visualize a safe, harmonious, and easy flight every day before you leave.

Earlier in the chapter we discussed how stress can disconnect us from ourselves and our loved ones. One profound result of mindfulness is the renewed and strengthened bonds we experience in our lives, community, and relationships. Practicing compassion and connection with ourselves in the present moment naturally leads to us extending that compassion and connection with others.

As you become accustomed to managing stress with mindfulness, you will find that stress has less of an effect on your mind and ADHD symptoms in general. This is of course due to brain training. When you make mindfulness habitual, you will find that you stay rooted in the present for longer and longer periods of time, and benefit from the clarity that comes with it.

Chapter 8
The Effects of ADHD on Childhood & Adolescence

We are going to pause briefly here in our mindfulness journey to take a deeper look into how ADHD presents in young children and teenagers. It's important to understand the differences in symptoms, behaviors, and risks of comorbidities. Maybe you are grappling with an adulthood diagnosis and are looking back on your childhood with a new understanding of your life's trajectory. Or perhaps you have kids in your life who have ADHD and need support. Whatever the reason, the more that is understood about ADHD in all stages of life, the easier it is to approach it with a mindfulness perspective.

MYTHS ABOUT ADHD & CHILDHOOD

Despite ADHD being more in the pop cultural consciousness than ever before, many myths about the disorder persist, and many of them disproportionately affect children. If you're a child trying to navigate the social hierarchies of school or a teenager struggling with academic pressure, these myths can be exceedingly harmful.

- **ADHD is not a real condition.** We have devoted an entire chapter to the neurological processes that result in ADHD. It is an observed, empirical fact that ADHD is a real disorder that is estimated to affect upwards of 20% of the population.

- **Only little boys have ADHD.** This myth is the result of a failure to understand the differences in the way in which ADHD presents in boys and girls. We will cover these differences shortly.

- **Children outgrow ADHD.** As has been previously discussed, most people diagnosed with ADHD in childhood in fact do not outgrow it at all, with as much as 80% still experiencing symptoms into adulthood.

- **ADHD can be cured.** As of now, there is no cure for ADHD, only medication that can help manage symptoms.

Misinformation and misunderstanding are harmful contributors to many of the common comorbidities associated with ADHD, including depression and anxiety. For children, these myths can be doubly difficult to deal with. Very often, children do not possess the means to express themselves, and do not have the social capital to advocate for themselves. Combatting these detrimental stereotypes by educating the public more fully will also help the gap in care that currently leaves so many who have ADHD undiagnosed. Since symptoms of ADHD develop by age twelve, young children, adolescents, and teenagers will benefit greatly.

SYMPTOMS & DIAGNOSIS IN YOUNG CHILDREN

Whereas diagnosing ADHD in adults is reliant on a physical exam and self-reporting of symptoms, the process is a little more rigorous for children and teenagers.

Diagnosing children with ADHD involves being assessed by a medical professional who follows a set of standardized guidelines developed by the American Academy of Pediatrics. Usually it is the child's primary care pediatrician, but neurologists, psychologists, and psychiatrists can also do a formal assessment.

The standard that needs to be met is pretty straightforward: six or more symptoms of hyperactivity and impulsiveness, six or more symptoms of attention deficit, or six or more symptom of a combination of the two need to be present on a regular basis, and for more than six months prior to diagnosis in at least two settings. The presence of the symptoms need to cause "severe" impairment in the child's life in areas such as schoolwork, relationships with parents and siblings, relationships with peers, and the ability to function in group settings like sports teams.

In order to assess that the standards for diagnosis are met in children, the physician or mental health professional will conduct interviews with at least one parent and at least one other caregiver who interacts with the child outside the home, such as a teacher, religious leader, or coach. It's important that the symptoms be observed in two settings because children and teens often behave differently in front of their families than they do in front of other authority figures. Different symptoms may also present themselves at school or elsewhere that could suggest a different root cause from ADHD.

A physical exam will also be done, and a doctor might refer the child to a behavioral or neurological specialist in order to rule out other disorders that share symptoms with ADHD. However, physical exams are not solely sufficient for diagnosis, due to the fact that brain chemistry is so individualized, particularly during the toddler years when the brain is rapidly developing.

The child's full medical history will also be considered in order to give current symptoms and behaviors context. For example, a child who has a history of febrile seizure may experience symptoms similar to ADHD in adolescence, even though they do not have ADHD.

Children as young as four years old can be diagnosed using these guidelines. It's extremely difficult to diagnose children younger than four years old, even if parents think they are showing symptoms of ADHD. As mentioned above, babies and young toddlers' brains develop and change incredibly quickly – the brain quite literally doubles in size during the first year of life – and behavior or symptoms that might exist one week, might not be present the next. Infants and toddlers younger than four years may also exhibit symptoms of ADHD due to sudden lifestyle change, such as a death in the family, a move, or parents divorcing, etc. By age four, though, the brain is nearly 90% developed, and most children are in some kind of preschool or group childcare. This makes diagnosis easier as symptoms tend to sustain and peer interactions can be observed by an adult other than the child's parent.

Symptoms of ADHD in early childhood include an inability to sit still (often called fidgeting), inability to focus on age appropriate tasks, becoming easily frustrated with age appropriate tasks, poor sleep habits and frequent night wakings, and rapid, often intense mood swings. Because these are all somewhat common and expected behaviors in young children in general, being able to assess the child's behavior and cognitive skills in relation to their peers is crucial.

One symptom that is often seen as out of the ordinary is the high number of dangerous, sometimes life threatening accidents that young children with ADHD are prone to have. Everything from burns to dental trauma is many times more common in children with ADHD when compared to their neuro-typical peers (Amiri et al., 2017). Additionally, children with ADHD have frontal cortices that are often cognitively delayed. This is known as the "Executive Age" and typically the ADHD brain is about 30% behind developmentally. This means that while a child with ADHD may be ten years old, their cognitive age will be seven years old and will display behaviors associated with the frontal cortex typically found in seven year olds.

SYMPTOMS & DIAGNOSIS IN ADOLESCENTS & TEENAGERS

The Executive Age disparity will last until a person's brain has fully developed, which typically happens between twenty-two and twenty-eight years old. For an ADHD brain, this could take longer. For teenagers, this can further complicate a season of life that is already defined by hormonal change and stress.

Like children, adolescents are diagnosed using the same three pronged approach of caregiver observations, at least two settings, and a physical exam. Teenagers, though, need to meet less criteria (five, rather than six). They are also similar to small children in that they can be somewhat harder to diagnose. Because so many of the symptoms of ADHD are difficult to distinguish from the normal behavior of their peers. Teenagers are notoriously moody, disorganized, and prone to emotional outbursts, but around the time someone with ADHD reaches adolescents, a new symptom is often introduced: hyper-focus.

Hyper-focus is defined by the ability to intensely focus on one or two activities, often to the detriment of other tasks and responsibilities. The normal symptoms of inattention, distractibility, or impulsivity seem to not get in the way of whatever the teenager is focusing on in the moment. There had been much speculation that many of history's great artistic masters had ADHD – Pablo Picasso and Vincent Van Gogh, for example, spoke and wrote about symptoms that seemed to indicate they could possibly have had the disorder – and many have talked about using hyper-focus as a tool in their craft. In this way, symptoms can be seen as a blessing, rather than frustrating.

However, in the case of adolescents, often what they hyper-focus on are activities or hobbies, such as video games, a particular music act, role play activities, etc. Because parents and other caregivers see that there is an *ability* to focus, the assumption is that the teenager just doesn't *want* to focus on more pressing things, like homework or household chores. This assumption is that a lack of willpower is the cause, rather than the actual cause, which is of course a developmental disorder.

Teens are also at risk for heightened comorbidities. While the usual symptoms are present, there is an increase in self-focused behavior, emotionality that can lead to rejection sensitive dysphoria (the feeling that they are being criticized or rejected by people they esteem), and poor decision making. These three symptoms in particular, acting in concert, can wreak havoc on teenage mental health, which is already struggling with an increase in hormonal activity as the brain fine-tunes cognitive functions as they near adulthood. Because of this, conduct that would be seen as normal or even healthy in the average teenager, can be exaggerated and dangerous in one with ADHD.

For example, one study found that an early and habitual use of drugs was nearly twice as likely in teenagers with ADHD; more than 40% drink alcohol before the age of fourteen, compared to 22% of their neuro-typical peers (Sinha, 2008). Additionally, teenagers with ADHD are more likely to have lower test scores, more likely to drop out of school, and have "regrettable instances of internet and/or social media use" (Sinha, 2008). One area that has been extensively studied, is the instance of car accidents and teenagers with ADHD. A Harvard review found that if an adolescent driver has ADHD, there is 62% higher rate of auto accidents resulting in injury, and an increase of 109% of accidents involving alcohol (McCarthy, 2019).

Crucially, none of the above behaviors are exhibited to such a great degree in adolescents with ADHD who are and have been on pharmaceutical medication. In fact, in some studies, the expressed behavioral changes and increases in medicated ADHD teens and adolescents were no different from that of their neuro-typical peers (Metzger & Sartin, 2022). Because of this, communication with a child's teachers, coaches, and other caregivers to ensure early diagnosis becomes critical. Luckily, the gap in care for ADHD is shrinking, and currently the average age of diagnosis is seven years old.

THE UNIQUE STRUGGLES & CHALLENGES

Particularly as children near and enter high school, the struggles that are often associated with ADHD can become exacerbated and overwhelming and symptoms will become amplified.

Peer pressure is difficult and uncomfortable for everyone, but for teenagers who are more likely to feel insecure in themselves, it can be a minefield. Teenagers with ADHD often miss social cues due to the symptoms of inattentiveness, making friendships more strained and difficult to navigate. An inability to relate to kids their age due to emotional dysregulation also plays a part, and this can increase feelings of isolation and loneliness, leading to depression.

Particularly in high school, academic pressure increases as teenagers prepare for college. For a teenager with ADHD, executive dysfunction can make it seem at times nearly impossible to focus in a classroom environment, and emotional dysregulation only makes the reaction to heightened stress worse. As we learned previously, stress and ADHD react off of each other to create a vicious cycle and feedback loop, which the young and still developing mind struggles with in particular.

This is also the time in life when there is an increased desire for independence. That their children will "act out" is a generally accepted reality for parents with teenagers, especially as they test boundaries and push against authority as they near adulthood. The impulsivity and hyper-activity of teens with ADHD can make these rebellions more dangerous, frequent, and intense. Hyper-focus and hyperactivity can also cause teens to lose interest in the activities that helped them compartmentalize in the past. For example, maybe a teenager played baseball, which required they practiced a mindful sort of meditation that helped with symptoms. If the teen stops playing baseball, they are no longer getting the benefits of the practice. This can cause a sudden appearance of previously unfelt symptoms, and lead to erratic behavior as the teenager tries to cope.

BOYS vs. GIRLS: THE CRUCIAL DIFFERENCES

For a long time, it was thought that ADHD only affected boys. This is because young and adolescent boys tend to display *externalized* symptoms of ADHD. Girls, on the other hand, have been found to display *internalized* symptoms.

The difference between externalized and internalized symptoms can be simply described as what can be observed, and what can't. If a child is showing symptoms of hyperactivity, it is easy to spot through their physical behavior, such as fidgeting, running, etc. These are externalized symptoms. However symptoms like stress and inattentiveness are harder to observe, and are generally only realized once self-reported. These are internalized symptoms.

It is not generally understood why girls tend to have more internalized symptoms, this difference has in the past meant that girls in comparison to boys, were critically underdiagnosed. In the 1990's, boys outpaced girls in ADHD diagnoses 9 to 1. In the last decade, though, that gap has closed considerably with 51% of childhood and adolescent diagnosis being boys, and 49% girls (Mahone, 2020). While treatment is important, it is critical to understand the increased risk girls are at for comorbidities and self-destructive behaviors.

Studies show that teen girls with ADHD are most likely to display sexually promiscuous behavior and more likely to contract sexually transmitted diseases or infections. They are also more likely to become pregnant unintentionally.

While all children and adolescents are more likely to suffer from anxiety, depression, and critically low self-esteem compared to their peers, girls with ADHD are more likely to react impulsively. Suicide attempts by girls with ADHD are reported at a rate of four times than that of girls without. Girls with ADHD are also two to three times more likely to report self-injury and purposefully harmful behavior than girls without.

SUPPORTING CHILDREN & ADOLESCENTS WITH ADHD

While all of this seems bleak, hopeless, and downright scary, there are ways to support and advocate for children and teens with ADHD. They are: Medication, Accommodation, and Participation, or *MAP*, an aptly named acronym as they will help kids and adolescents with ADHD chart a course to a happier, healthier, and less stressful childhood.

Medications and their benefits have already been discussed extensively in previous chapters, but it should be underscored that the earlier a child is medicated for ADHD, the less likely they are to ever experience the most severe comorbidities.

Accommodation in a school setting is provided for under two federal laws, the Individuals with Disabilities of Education Act and the Federal Rehabilitation Act. They generally take the form of an Independent Education Plan (IEP) or a 504 Plan, so named for the section it falls under in the Rehabilitation Act. IEPs are ideal for kids who experience ADHD in addition to other disorders, such as Autism, Oppositional Defiant Syndrome, or learning disabilities. 504 Plans are generally speaking more suited to kids who experience ADHD only. Under the law, public schools are not allowed to discriminate against any child with mental impairments that make learning in a classroom more difficult. The same way schools must provide handicap bathrooms, handicap lockers, and ramps for kids with physical impairments, they must provide accommodation for kids with ADHD. This accommodation can look like:

- Extra time on tests

- Instruction and assignments tailored to the child

- Using technology to assist with tasks

- Allowing breaks or time to move around

- Changes to the environment to limit distraction

- Extra help with staying organized

Receiving accommodation is a process. First, proof of the impairment needs to be submitted. If the child has not been diagnosed with ADHD, a school evaluation team can be requested. Second, either an IEP or 504 plan will be chosen based on what best caters to the child's needs under the law. Third, a customized plan will be developed for the child that includes classroom and instruction modification and also goals and milestones for the child to reach. For example, parents and teachers of the child might set a goal that classroom disruptions decrease month over month, and outline specifically how that will be accomplished. Fourth, progress will be monitored by both teachers and parents to make sure that the accommodation is beneficial.

The **Participation** of parents is crucial for kids with ADHD. Not only does it provide emotional support but can also teach kids how to advocate for themselves and set examples of behavior. Examples of participation can be positive reinforcement and praising good behaviors, involvement in academic life and extracurriculars, knowing where and who the child is with, and taking an interest in the child's inner life through open and loving communication.

In the next chapter we are going to discuss in detail the ways in which parents can use mindfulness to be active participants in their children's lives.

Chapter 9
Mindful Parenting for Children with ADHD

P arenting is a challenge under the absolute best of circumstances. Trying to be the best parent possible to a child with ADHD can be brutal. As we learned from the previous chapter, symptoms and challenges vary not only from child to child, but also from age group to age group. This makes establishing routines and setting expectations for your child very difficult. For a parent of a child with ADHD, it can feel as though as soon as you've got it all figured out or have finally developed a system for co-managing your child's symptoms, the game changes entirely and the rug is once again swept out from under you.

It's emotional whiplash, and the parents of children with ADHD face the very real, and even very likely, possibility that their own mental health will suffer. A 2019 study published in the *International Journal of Qualitative Studies on Health and Well-being* found that parents of children with ADHD are more likely to endure levels of stress that require professional support, more likely to end up divorced, more likely to face social stigma, and report feeling disconnected from and resentment toward their child (Leitch, et al., 2019), which can result in tremendous feelings of guilt and depression.

Another factor for parents to consider is the role genetics play in the presence of ADHD in their children.

71

In 2019 scholarly review was done of studies on the heritability of ADHD due to gene association. After reviewing one hundred seventy-three studies, the researchers found conclusively that "DNA variants in genes [...] increase the risk for ADHD" and that in some cases, children have an 80% chance of inheriting ADHD from a parent who has been diagnosed with the disorder (Faraone & Larsson, 2019). Because ADHD is assumed to be vastly underdiagnosed, it follows that parents who have children with ADHD could very well have it themselves and not know it. This would make emotional regulation, which is already so difficult when parenting, exceedingly mentally taxing.

The trials and tribulations of parenthood are magnified tenfold when parenting a child with ADHD. Children of course can be impulsive, emotionally volatile, and easily distracted even without developmental disorders. That being said, however, the frustrations that come with parenting an ADHD child are unique, and require a deep understanding of both your child and the disorder to be able to parent with compassion and confidence. The same study from Leicht, et al., further suggested that if parents could find the right mechanisms of support, then their personal, home, and family life would likely drastically improve – even if the child's ADHD never did. Luckily, in recent years, resources for the parents of children with ADHD have become more widely available.

One tried and true method is, of course, mindful meditation.

In previous chapters we developed our working definition of mindfulness as the practice of being a passive, non-judgemental observer to our own being in order to see ourselves as we are in the present moment. We are going to tweak that definition just a bit in order to better apply it to parenting. Once we have our definition, we can begin to consider the ways in which children with ADHD need support and how mindful parenting can provide it.

Mindful parenting means showing up for your child completely and understanding that the present moment is forever a chance to connect and grow together. It also means accepting that you are human and will make mistakes, react to situations and challenges emotionally, and sometimes disappoint your kid. When this happens, mindfulness teaches parents to take a step back and not linger with negative emotions, but to lead with calm objectivity. To put it more succinctly, *mindful parenting is being present in the moment with your child and viewing every situation without judgment.*

At times it can seem that it is especially difficult for parents to shed the weighty burden of judgment and perfectionism. Popular culture very often likes to tell parents everything they're doing is wrong, and social media can seem like a highlight reel of parents who always seem to be better, kinder, cleaner, and more together than you. There is so much pressure and expectation, that when the inevitable mistakes happen, it can lead to crushing guilt and anxiety.

But it's important to remember that it is not your job to be a perfect parent. Your job as a parent is to guide your children into being well-rounded, well-adjusted, and healthy adults. This feels easier said than done, of course, and ADHD will always throw a couple of curve balls into the mix.

73

SUPPORTING CHILDREN THROUGH INATTENTION WITH MINDFUL PARENTING

Children with ADHD have a hard road to walk. The ways that children experience the symptoms of ADHD can cause them to feel burdensome, that they can't do anything right, that they're letting people down, and that they're not "good". It's up to parents to protect their kids' mental health and mindfulness is a great way to do so.

The attention deficit part of attention deficit hyperactivity disorder is often sighted as the most frustrating symptom of ADHD. For adults, symptoms of inattention can be an inability to multitask or focus, and a poor working memory. In kids, particularly in girls, inattention can often look like willful misbehavior or spaciness. This can come across as easily distracted, not following directions, and in need of repeated reminders to finish even basic tasks. For parents, this can be incredibly frustrating. It's important to remember, however, that these symptoms are equally frustrating for the child, and reacting with those feelings of frustration in the form of harsh punishments or language will not "fix" the child, but instead sow seeds of resentment and mistrust.

Instead, using mindfulness to help guide your kid will keep you both calm, as well as model compassion and patience. Using guided visualization is a great way to get kids focused and motivated. It has many benefits, but does two things in particular that are important for young minds:

- It sets clear expectations without using threats.

- Motivates and guides using gentle and positive direction, ie: "do this" versus "don't do that."

74

Let's use a real-world example to show the method in action.

Your kid's room is messy. There are toys and clothes everywhere. Their schoolbooks are scattered on their desk and their bed needs to be made. You have told them several times now that the room needs to be cleaned, but they keep getting distracted. You find yourself getting frustrated and you don't understand why it can't just get *done.*

You could use threats to try to motivate: "Pick up the toys or I am throwing them all in the trash!" You could also point out what they're doing wrong: "Stop dawdling! You're not doing what I asked!" Or, you could use judgmental language: "What is wrong with you? Just get it done, it shouldn't take this long!"

Instead of letting your negative emotions act as the parent, take a moment to view the situation objectively: the room is messy. That's it. Nothing more or less. Luckily, your kid is not a bad kid for having trouble focusing, you're not a bad parent for feeling frustrated. Further, a messy room is not a moral quandary; it's just a chore that needs to get done.

After you feel grounded, calmly have your child follow you to a quieter area of your home and ask them to sit and breathe with you for a moment. Tell them that you want to help them get motivated and focused to clean their room by imagining with them what the room will look like when it's clean, and how good it will feel when the chore is all done. Start with something easy. For instance, "Picture us pulling all the sheets off your bed and the pillowcase off your pillow and putting them in the hamper" or "

Slowly and patiently walk your child through the process of cleaning their room. Describe how each cleaned mess or newly tidied area will make their room so much more relaxing and fun to be in. "Once all your books are put away, it will be so much easier to find your favorites and we can read them together." Have them visualize themselves completing the task and tell them how good it will feel when they're done. "You will feel so good once it's all done and you have room to dance around on the floor" or, "Nice clean sheets are the best!"

This is a great exercise to do with younger children. As they grow, reverse the meditation, and ask them to visualize and guide you through getting grounded and focusing. Once they are teenagers, they will probably visualize themselves accomplishing tasks and finishing projects, even things like competing in sporting events or learning to play a musical instrument, all on their own.

Visualization is a powerful tool used by artists, CEOs, and professional athletes. Simone Biles, who has ADHD and is arguably the greatest gymnast in history, told *Vanity Fair* that her training secret is visualization (Taylor, 2016). Teaching your ADHD child visualization is adding a mindfulness tool to their life skills toolbox.

SUPPORTING CHILDREN THROUGH HYPERACTIVITY WITH MINDFUL PARENTING

Hyperactivity is oftentimes, and especially for boys, the first sign for caregivers that a child may have ADHD. Hyperactivity conjures to the mind a picture of an overly rambunctious child, wreaking havoc by ceaseless yelling and running around wildly. While these are certainly behaviors commonly associated with hyperactivity, the symptom can also present as a child making careless mistakes by rushing through tasks, inappropriate behavior for the time and place, and fidgeting.

Parenting a hyperactive child can be exhausting, particularly when it seems that nothing will ever get the child to calm down or stop moving. Because of this, mindfulness techniques that require stillness are likely going to cause more frustration. Instead, try mindful movements with your kid, such as yoga.

Children who practice yoga have been shown to focus better and longer, show increased awareness, and have a better memory. According to a 2016 Harvard Health article, yoga also boosts self-esteem, and improves classroom behavior in school age children. It has many physical benefits for children as well, including increased strength, balance, endurance, and aerobic capacity (Wei, 2016). Perhaps most interesting to parents of hyperactive kids is the keen awareness of their bodies that children develop from even just five minutes of yoga a day.

To begin yoga practice with your child, try incorporating two short sequences into the daily routine. Maybe it makes sense to do five minutes in the morning, and then five minutes before bed. Perhaps your child would best benefit from yoga right after they get home from school or directly after doing homework. You know your kid best, so the timing is entirely up to you. Here are some tips to ensure that no matter when you and your child do yoga together, it is a fun and centering time of connection for you both.

- Make sure that the sequence of poses you have put together are age appropriate and won't be difficult for your child to do. Mastering the poses will boost confidence, but even more simply, kids (and all people, really) like to do things they're good at. Your kid is more likely to want to make yoga a habit if they know they can do it well. Here are some great poses that are perfect for beginners as young as two years old:

- o Mountain pose

- o Raised hands pose

- o Modified Warrior 2

- o Cobra pose

- o Downward facing dog

- o Cat & Cow

- o Modified Lotus pose

- o Savasana or Corpse pose

- Start small and scale up. As we know, even adults with ADHD can have a very difficult time focusing for extended periods of time, and we've recommended mindfulness practices such as meditation only last a couple of minutes in the beginning. With young kids, go even smaller. Begin and end yoga with ten seconds of quiet time in which their eyes are closed. When you feel your kid is ready, add two seconds.

- As you move through the poses with them, remind them to be attuned with their body. You can do this by asking questions: "Do you feel your feet flat on the floor? Do you feel your muscles stretching?" Or by modeling awareness yourself. "I like how long my arms feel when we do raised arms pose."

- Encourage kids to speak openly about their inner selves by checking in with them at the end of the practice. All yoga sequences traditionally end with Savasana, or Corpse pose. When your child is laying on their back on the floor, you can ask them how they're feeling, how they want their day to go/how it went, if they feel restless or stressed. Particularly with younger children, this is an ideal time to incorporate physical affection, which is vital for kids, by holding their hand or stroking their hair.

Remember not to bring expectation into your practice, for your child or for yourself. Think of yoga as a chance to connect and move your body without putting on pressure for a perfect outcome.

SUPPORTING CHILDREN THROUGH IMPULSIVITY WITH MINDFUL PARENTING

Parenting children with ADHD can be an emotional minefield, particularly when trying to navigate how to best support them through instances of impulsiveness. Impulsivity is incredibly difficult for children to deal with, not only because it can get them in trouble with their parents, teacher, and other authority figures, but also because it often makes them an outcast amongst their peers. Behaviors commonly associated with impulsivity can include: constantly interrupting or blurting things out, doing things they know they shouldn't, and trouble sharing or taking turns. One of the hardest symptoms of impulsivity is the tendency to be effusively emotional. This can mean throwing tantrums that don't seem to fit with the trigger, or laughing excessively and loudly long after everyone else has stopped.

These symptoms can bring up feelings of embarrassment and shame in children, but also in their parents. These feelings are natural, and you should feel no guilt if they arise in you. Instead accept that sometimes kids (all kids) are embarrassing, and do not project your embarrassment onto your child. Remember, you are responsible for protecting their sense of self-worth because they do not have the tools to do so yet.

Mindful meditation is a fantastic way to decrease impulsive behavior, but it can be difficult to teach it to children. We will instead modify the practice and teach children to be grounded in the moment by using breathing exercises and the five senses.

For children with ADHD, particularly young children, learning to pause and take a breath will be an invaluable life-long skill. For little kids, there is a fun and easy exercise you can do with them that will help them become aware of their breath.

Take a feather (feathers can be purchased at any craft store) and set it in front of you on a table. Show your child how you are going to take a deep breath in, and then blow it out, and the feather will fly across the table. Demonstrate this to them a couple of times, and then ask them to do it. Count to three as they breathe in and then praise them as they blow it out, no matter how far the feather goes. Point out how their chest expands with they breathe in, how their shoulders drop when they breathe out. Practice this at home when you can see your child struggling with impulsiveness and you find yourself getting frustrated. "I feel myself getting frustrated, and I think the feather game will help me feel better." When your kid has mastered this, you can take it out into the world by reminding them of the feather game and asking them to show them their big breaths.

For older children, the feather game might seem too juvenile. Instead, go on a walk together. While outside, ask them to focus their hearing, sight, sense of smell, taste, and touch to describe the world around them. When they describe a sensation, ask them how that sensation makes them feel, what immediate emotions arise in them when they see or hear or otherwise experience certain stimuli.

Don't be afraid of the conversation feeling awkward. Starting something new will always be a process. Eventually, you and your kid will be able to walk and experience the present moment together effortlessly. The bond you will create from this connection will be worth any temporary uncomfortableness.

TECHNIQUES TO INCORPORATE MINDFULNESS INTO PARENTING ROUTINES

Now that you know how to support your child, let's take a moment to discuss how you can show up for yourself with mindfulness as you navigate the hardest job in the world – being a parent. Below we've compiled four tips that can be used every day that will help you live in the present.

- **Make time for you to experience your emotions.** Emotions, while not facts, are valid and a vital, often beautiful part, of the human experience. Not only that, but the only way to process emotions is by feeling them fully. Set aside time each day to do just that, even if it's for just a few moments. You will be more regulated, more centered, and more present for your child when you do.

- **Practice acceptance.** Acceptance has been a huge theme throughout this guide, and with good reason. Only by accepting our limitations, emotions, fears, and insecurities can we really move past them. Denial allows things to fester and grow. Remember the adage from previous chapters: *What we resist will persist.*

- **Let go of the idea of control and embrace flexibility.** To crave control is to be human. Control allows us to face the future with a certain measure of predictability and to feel comforted by rigidity. But, as anyone who has been in the presence of a child for more than a few hours will tell you, the best laid plans can and will go awry. Rather than clinging to a false sense of control, embrace that you are not in control and still you are here, in the moment, with your child.

- Make gratitude a verb. The idea of practicing gratitude is a powerful one. It keeps us focused on the things that matter and helps cultivate a sense of compassion. It's also a wonderful thing to pass on to your children. You can practice gratitude in any number of ways; by keeping a gratitude journal, by meditating on the things you are grateful for, or by speaking your gratitude aloud.

ENHANCING EMOTIONAL CONNECTION & COMMUNICATION WITH CHILDREN WITH MINDFULNESS

Practicing mindfulness with your kid or supporting your kid as they learn to practice mindfulness themselves, can deepen the bond between a parent and child. Due to their young age, the uniquely malleable nature of their minds, and their lack of bad habits to unlearn, children are primed to practice mindfulness. The best way for a child to learn mindfulness is to see it exhibited by their parent or caregiver. Parents can use these strategies to demonstrate mindful connection.

- **Be present.** Put away all distractions and focus on your child. Make eye contact and smile. Engage them in conversation and talk openly with them about what you're feeling in the moment.

- **Stay calm.** When you and your child must navigate a tense or frustrating moment, try to acknowledge the feeling without becoming outwardly irritated. This can create a vicious cycle in which parent and child feed off each other's agitation.

- **Implement S.T.O.P.** If the feeling of frustration grows to the point where you are feeling disconnected from your child and the moment, use the STOP method from chapter 4 to recenter yourself.

When you are considering what kinds of mindfulness practices to try when you want to strengthen emotional bonds, consider loving-kindness meditation. Loving-kindness emphasizes compassion for oneself and others, which is vital for parenting children with ADHD.

Compassion breeds patience for the child and grace for yourself. It also gives you permission to adjust expectations, manage your own feelings, and ensure that you won't project any anger or feelings of helplessness and guilt onto your child.

As discussed in previous chapters, owning your emotions means that your emotions cannot own you. Mindful meditation is ideal for parents who find their own emotional responses can become dysregulated due to the high stress associated with raising a child with ADHD. When a non-judgmental acceptance of the present is prioritized, it means that you are no longer ruled by your emotions and are free to connect with, support, protect, and love your child.

Incorporating mindful meditation into your parenting will also build trust. Your child needs to know that they are not going to be held responsible for your behavior, and that their thoughts, emotions, and fears are safe with you. Children who trust their parents and feel unconditional love from them are happier and report less instances of toxic stress. It also helps with emotional regulation when a child knows they are getting the support at home. Trust also builds a sense of security, which is vital for brain development. (Ying et al., 2015)

While parenting will never be easy, and parenting children with ADHD is particularly hard, it's important for parents to know that there are mindfulness strategies that can help. What we've covered here only scratches the surface but will provide a strong foundation for you and your child as you navigate the challenges of ADHD together.

Conclusion

Congratulations! You've completed our guide on the power of meditation for attention deficit hyperactivity disorder. Our mission was to provide you with a concise and accurate understanding of what ADHD is, how it influences the brain, how those influences present as symptoms, and how mindful meditation can help manage those symptoms. It is our belief, backed by science, that meditation in concert with pharmaceutical treatments can drastically improve the quality of life for those who suffer from ADHD.

First, we learned that ADHD is a developmental disorder that currently affects about 5% of the adult population and about 9% of children. It's caused by a chemical imbalance in the brain and affects four major cognitive areas that deal mainly with attentiveness, impulsive behaviors, and emotional regulation. We learned about the comorbidities of ADHD and also that the symptoms can be debilitating. We learned about medications, both stimulants and non-stimulants, and how they only negligibly help with emotional regulation.

Next, we began our mindfulness journey. There is a wealth of scientific literature that proves mindfulness not only supports the mind emotionally, but also architecturally and we delved deeper into some of these studies to understand how. In chapter 4 we explored some different types of mindfulness and how they can be used to help manage ADHD symptoms. We went over how to set up an ideal meditation space and how to begin a meditation routine. We discussed different ways to use mindfulness during in-the-moment instances of emotional dysregulation, inattentiveness, or impulsivity. We spent time thinking about cultivating emotional resilience, particularly when related to stress, a chemical reaction in the emotional center of the brain that recent research suggests has a vicious cycle relationship with ADHD.

Finally, we discussed ADHD in different life stages and how it can present differently depending upon age, sex, and individual brain chemistry. From there we learned powerful ways to use mindfulness as a parent – both to support your child and yourself.

It's been our goal from the beginning to offer motivation, practical and actionable steps, as well as hope to anyone with ADHD who finds themselves continually frustrated, stressed and struggling with their self-worth. While ADHD is becoming more mainstream, myths surrounding the disorder persist and it can feel helpless and lonely when trying to manage your symptoms on your own. It was with that in mind that we wrote this guide, to offer mindful support and loving guidance. We hope you enjoyed reading it and will continue to benefit from it for a long time to come.

Dear Reader,

Thank you for joining us on this wonderful journey through the pages of this book: "The Power of Meditation for ADHD: A Guide to Managing ADHD Symptoms with Mindful Meditation". If you enjoyed reading this book and found the content helpful, please leave us a kind and honest review on Amazon.

To leave a review directly on Amazon, please scan the QR code below. Thank you.

References

ADHD and Youth Suicide: Is There a Link? (n.d.). https://www.nationwidechildrens.org/family-resources-education/700childrens/2019/08/adhd-and-youth-suicide

ADHD in Children. (2004, June 30). WebMD. https://www.webmd.com/add-adhd/childhood-adhd/adhd-children#

Agarwal, R. (n.d.). *The Quality of Life of Adults with Attention Deficit Hyperactivity Disorder: A Systematic Review.* PubMed Central (PMC). https://www.ncbi.nlm.nih.gov/pmc/articles/PMC3398685/

Amiri, S., Sadeghi-Bazargani, H., Nazari, S., Ranjbar, F., & Abdi, S. (2017). Attention deficit/hyperactivity disorder and risk of injuries: a systematic review and meta-analysis. *Journal of Injury and Violence Research, 9*(2). https://doi.org/10.5249/jivr.v9i2.858

Bigelow, H., Gottlieb, M. D., Ogrodnik, M., Graham, J. B., & Fenesi, B. (2021). The Differential Impact of Acute Exercise and Mindfulness Meditation on Executive Functioning and Psycho-Emotional Well-Being in Children and Youth With ADHD. *Frontiers in Psychology, 12.* https://doi.org/10.3389/fpsyg.2021.660845

CDC. (2022, April 19). *ADHD in the Classroom.* Centers for Disease Control and Prevention. https://www.cdc.gov/ncbddd/adhd/school-success.html

Department of Health & Human Services. (n.d.). *Sleep deprivation.* Better Health Channel. https://www.betterhealth.vic.gov.au/health/conditionsandtreatments/sleep-deprivation

Dijk, D., & Czeisler, C. A. (1995). Contribution of the circadian pacemaker and the sleep homeostat to sleep propensity, sleep structure, electroencephalographic slow waves, and sleep spindle activity in humans. *The Journal of Neuroscience, 15*(5), 3526–3538. https://doi.org/10.1523/jneurosci.15-05-03526.1995

Dupuy, P. (2013, June 29). *How to Develop Compassion: The 5 Stages of Loving Kindness Meditation.* iAwake Technologies. https://www.iawaketechnologies.com/how-to-develop-compassion-the-5-stages-of-loving-kindness-meditation/

Elizsross. (2020, November 1). *15 Relatable ADHD Memes to Brighten Your Day - SMARTS.* SMARTS. https://smarts-ef.org/blog/15-relatable-adhd-memes-to-brighten-your-day/

Faraone, S. V., & Larsson, H. (2019a). Genetics of attention deficit hyperactivity disorder. *Molecular Psychiatry, 24*(4), 562–575. https://doi.org/10.1038/s41380-018-0070-0

Faraone, S. V., & Larsson, H. (2019b). Genetics of attention deficit hyperactivity disorder. *Molecular Psychiatry, 24*(4), 562–575. https://doi.org/10.1038/s41380-018-0070-0

Gender Myths & ADHD - CHADD. (2021, September 30). CHADD. https://chadd.org/adhd-news/adhd-news-educators/gender-myths-adhd/

Gerten, K. (2021). Relax! How to Be a More Mindful Parent. *Youth Dynamics.* https://www.youthdynamics.org/dont-bark-the-art-of-mindful-parenting/

Ghavami, T., Kazeminia, M., & Rajati, F. (2022). The effect of lavender on stress in individuals: A systematic review and meta-analysis. *Complementary Therapies in Medicine, 68,* 102832. https://doi.org/10.1016/j.ctim.2022.102832

Hamilton, A. (2012, August 14). Girls With ADHD At Risk for Self-Injury, Suicide Attempts As Young Adults, Says New Research. *https://www.apa.org.* https://www.apa.org/news/press/releases/2012/08/girls-adhd#

Hasan, S. H. (n.d.). *Parenting a Child with ADHD.* Kids Health. https://kidshealth.org/en/parents/parenting-kid-adhd.html

How Meditation Affects Your Brain and Boosts Well-Being. (2021, January 27). Right as Rain by UW Medicine. https://rightasrain.uwmedicine.org/mind/well-being/science-behind-meditation

How US children are diagnosed with ADHD. (2018, September 28). Centers for Disease Control and Prevention. https://www.cdc.gov/ncbddd/adhd/features/how-us-children-diagnosed.html

Ireland, T. (2014, June 12). *What Does Mindfulness Meditation Do to Your Brain?* Scientific American Blog Network. https://blogs.scientificamerican.com/guest-blog/what-does-mindfulness-meditation-do-to-your-brain/#

Janove, J., JD. (2021, July 6). ADHD in the Workplace. *SHRM.* https://www.shrm.org/resourcesandtools/hr-topics/employee-relations/humanity-into-hr/pages/adhd-in-the-workplace.aspx

Kang, D. H., Jo, H. J., Jung, W. H., Kim, S., Jung, Y. L., Choi, C. K., Lee, U. S., An, S. H., Jang, J. H., & Kwon, J. S. (2013). The effect of meditation on brain structure: cortical thickness mapping and diffusion tensor imaging. *Social Cognitive and Affective Neuroscience, 8*(1), 27–33. https://doi.org/10.1093/scan/nss056

Kelly, K. (2022, September 21). *7 Ways to Meditate with a Busy Brain* [Video]. ADDitude. https://www.additudemag.com/how-to-meditate-adhd-brain-video/

Kjaer, T. W., Bertelsen, C., Piccini, P., Brooks, D. J., Alving, J., & Lou, H. C. (2002). Increased dopamine tone during meditation-induced change of consciousness. *Cognitive Brain Research, 13*(2), 255–259. https://doi.org/10.1016/s0926-6410(01)00106-9

Korponay, C., Dentico, D., Kral, T. R. A., Ly, M., Kruis, A., Davis, K., Goldman, R. I., Lutz, A., & Davidson, R. J. (2019). The Effect of Mindfulness Meditation on Impulsivity and its Neurobiological Correlates in Healthy Adults. *Scientific Reports, 9*(1). https://doi.org/10.1038/s41598-019-47662-y

Leitch, S., Sciberras, E., Post, B., Gerner, B., Rinehart, N. J., Nicholson, J. M., & Evans, S. (2019). Experience of stress in parents of children with ADHD: A qualitative study. *International Journal of Qualitative Studies on Health and Well-being, 14*(1), 1690091. https://doi.org/10.1080/17482631.2019.1690091

Lf-Apa, W. D. M. (2023, May 24). *How ADHD Ignites Rejection Sensitive Dysphoria.* ADDitude. https://www.additudemag.com/rejection-sensitive-dysphoria-and-adhd/

Mahone, E. M., PhD. (2020, November 16). Neuropsychiatric Differences Between Boys and Girls With ADHD. *Psychiatric Times.* https://www.psychiatrictimes.com/view/neuropsychiatric-differences-between-boys-and-girls-adhd

Managing Stress When You Have ADHD. (2019, October 18). CHADD. https://chadd.org/adhd-weekly/managing-stress-when-you-have-adhd/

McCarthy, C., MD. (2019). Driving for teens with ADHD: What parents need to know. *Harvard Health.* https://www.health.harvard.edu/blog/teens-with-adhd-and-driving-what-parents-need-to-know-2019083017633

Metzger, K., & Sartin, E. (2022, April 19). *Examining How and Why Teens with ADHD Crash.* Center for Injury Research and Prevention. https://injury.research.chop.edu/blog/posts/examining-how-and-why-teens-adhd-crash

Mindfulness for Children. (n.d.). Well Guides - the New York Times. https://www.nytimes.com/guides/well/mindfulness-for-children

Mindfulness meditation: A research-proven way to reduce stress. (2019, October 30). *https://www.apa.org.* https://www.apa.org/topics/mindfulness/meditation

Pacheco, D., & Pacheco, D. (2023). ADHD and Sleep. *Sleep Foundation.* https://www.sleepfoundation.org/mental-health/adhd-and-sleep

Patel, A. K. (2022, September 7). *Physiology, Sleep Stages.* StatPearls - NCBI Bookshelf. https://www.ncbi.nlm.nih.gov/books/NBK526132/

Pizzoli, S. F. M., Monzani, D., Mazzocco, K., Maggioni, E., & Pravettoni, G. (2021). The Power of Odor Persuasion: The Incorporation of Olfactory Cues in Virtual Environments for Personalized Relaxation. *Perspectives on*

Psychological Science, *17*(3), 652–661. https://doi.org/10.1177/17456916211014196

Plessen, K. J., Bansal, R., Zhu, H., Whiteman, R., Amat, J., V., Quackenbush, G., Martin, L. E., Durkin, K. A., Blair, C., Royal, J., Hugdahl, K., & Peterson, B. S. (2006). Hippocampus and Amygdala Morphology in Attention-Deficit/Hyperactivity Disorder. *Archives of General Psychiatry*, *63*(7), 795. https://doi.org/10.1001/archpsyc.63.7.795

Preschoolers and ADHD - CHADD. (2018, May 25). CHADD. https://chadd.org/for-parents/preschoolers-and-adhd/

Ross, A. (2016, March 9). How Meditation Went Mainstream. *Time*. https://time.com/4246928/meditation-history-buddhism/

Seven Ways to Help Kids Build a Lifelong Yoga Practice. (n.d.). Kripalu. https://kripalu.org/resources/seven-ways-help-kids-build-lifelong-yoga-practice

Signs and symptoms of stress. (n.d.). Mind. https://www.mind.org.uk/information-support/types-of-mental-health-problems/stress/signs-and-symptoms-of-stress/

Sinha, R. (2008). Chronic Stress, Drug Use, and Vulnerability to Addiction. *Annals of the New York Academy of Sciences*, *1141*(1), 105–130. https://doi.org/10.1196/annals.1441.030

Skogli, E. W., Teicher, M. H., Andersen, P. K., Hovik, K. T., & Øie, M. G. (2013). ADHD in girls and boys – gender differences in co-existing symptoms and executive function measures. *BMC Psychiatry*, *13*(1). https://doi.org/10.1186/1471-244x-13-298

Taren, A. A., Creswell, J. D., & Gianaros, P. J. (2013). Dispositional Mindfulness Co-Varies with Smaller Amygdala and Caudate Volumes in Community Adults. *PLOS ONE*, *8*(5), e64574. https://doi.org/10.1371/journal.pone.0064574

Taylor, E. (2016, August 11). A Brief Encounter With Simone Biles on Her Way to Olympic Gold. *Vanity Fair*. https://www.vanityfair.com/culture/2016/08/simone-biles-olympic-gold-medal-before

The Color of the Light Affects the Circadian Rhythms | NIOSH | CDC. (n.d.). https://www.cdc.gov/niosh/emres/longhourstraining/color.html

Wei, M., MD JD. (2016). More than just a game: Yoga for school-age children. *Harvard Health*. https://www.health.harvard.edu/blog/more-than-just-a-game-yoga-for-school-age-children-201601299055

Wolraich, M. L., Hagan, J., Allan, C. C., Chan, E., Davison, D., Earls, M. F., Evans, S. W., Flinn, S. K., Froehlich, T. E., Frost, J. J., Holbrook, J. D., Lehmann, C. U., Lessin, H. R., Okechukwu, K., Pierce, K., Winner, J. D., Zurhellen, W., Children, S. O., & Disorder, H. (2019). ADHD: Clinical Practice Guideline for the Diagnosis, Evaluation, and Treatment of Attention-

Deficit/Hyperactivity Disorder in Children and Adolescents. *Pediatrics*, *128*(5), 1007–1022. https://doi.org/10.1542/peds.2011-2654

World Health Organization. (2022, June 17). *Stress*. https://www.who.int/news-room/questions-and-answers/item/stress

Ying, L., Ma, F., Huang, H., Guo, X., Chen, C., & Xu, F. (2015). Parental Monitoring, Parent-Adolescent Communication, and Adolescents' Trust in Their Parents in China. *PLOS ONE*, *10*(8), e0134730. https://doi.org/10.1371/journal.pone.0134730

Zimmaro, L. A., Moss, A. S., Reibel, D. K., Handorf, E., Reese, J. B., & Temel, J. S. (2021). A Telephone-Adapted Mindfulness-Based Stress Reduction Program: Preliminary Effects among Healthcare Employees. *Behavioral Sciences*, *11*(10), 139. https://doi.org/10.3390/bs11100139

Zwarensteyn, J. (2023). Is It Really Better To Sleep in a Cold Room? *Sleep Advisor*. https://www.sleepadvisor.org/sleeping-in-a-cold-room/

Printed in Great Britain
by Amazon

36281097R00056